Empowerment

The Art of Creating
Your Life As You Want It

David Gershon

and

Gail Straub

Delta
Trade Paperbacks

A Delta Book

Published by Dell Publishing
a division of
Bantam Doubleday Dell Publishing Group, Inc.
1540 Broadway
New York, New York 10036

Illustrations by Isa Trapani © 1989
Photographs © by Haroldo de Faria Castro

"Partners" from DOES GOD HAVE A BIG TOE? STORIES ABOUT STORIES
IN THE BIBLE by Marc Gellman. HarperCollins, October 1989.

Library of Congress Cataloging in Publication Data

Gershon, David.
    Empowerment / David Gershon and Gail Straub.
        p.   cm.
    Bibliography: p.
    ISBN 0-385-29772-6
    I. Self-realization.   2. Visualization.   I. Straub, Gail.
II. Title.
BF637.S4G47   1989   89-7744
158'.1—dc20   CIP

Printed in the United States of America
Published simultaneously in Canada

November 1989

10 9

KPP

Acknowledgments

We would like to express our gratitude to the Empowerment Workshop graduates all over the world whose commitment to personal growth have added depth and compassion to the teachings in this book. We especially acknowledge those graduates whose personal stories are used in the book. Pseudonyms have been used for all such stories.

Special thanks are due to those friends who patiently reviewed the manuscript: Elizabeth Rose Campbell, Diane Davis, Kathryn Hendren, and Ned Leavitt. Their careful reading and obvious caring were deeply appreciated.

Finally we would like to thank the people who contributed to the creation of the book: Anne Marie O'Farrell, our agent, for her indomitable spirit; Isa Trapani, our illustrator, for her wonderful and heartwarming drawings; and Dawson Church and Jody Rein for their invaluable editorial efforts.

Contents

Empowerment

Prologue

On a January evening in 1981 we were in Arnold's Turtle, one of our favorite restaurants in Manhattan, discussing our future life together. We had met in the autumn, fallen in love, and decided to get married. As we were eating we got into one of our many marathon talks about our future.

The subject of work came up, and we realized that the common purpose of the workshops we each were leading individually was to assist people in becoming more empowered. At that time *empowerment* was not a very common word, but we were both struck by the fact that it was the primary idea underlying our philosophies of teaching. We realized at that moment that one of the reasons we had come together was to combine what we had each learned about empowerment into a coherent body of knowledge and present it in the form of an intensive personal growth workshop. That's how we each came to the point of creating the Empowerment Workshop upon which this book is based.

For me, Gail, it was my parents who first set the tone for my path of growing and learning. From my mother I received a profound love and curiosity about spirituality and the inner life. Her spiritual life was rich, and she had a remarkable capacity to impart a love of spirit without guilt or heavy dogma. As a child I loved talking to her about guardian angels, God, and why the sky was so blue. She taught me about love by the way she lived. She was one of the most loving presences I have ever known.

From my father I received a sense of social responsibility and a yearning to create a better world. Very early he taught me to ask, "Why is the world out of balance? . . . What can I do about it?" He encouraged me to find my own answers and to know that my actions counted. He was a man of rare integrity and he taught me to base my choices in life upon this quality.

The blending of these two precious gifts—the path of spirit walked by my mother and the path of action walked by my father—has continued to be the major theme of my life.

I was also blessed by the education I received between the ages of five and eighteen. It gave balanced attention to the mental, emotional, physical, and spiritual aspects of learning. Though I didn't realize it until many years later, this education imbued me with the understanding that the learning process is a holistic, multidimensional experience.

A major rite of passage in my life had to do with living in different cultures. By the time I was twenty-four I had lived and worked in South

America, Europe, and Africa. Each was a significant classroom, and I developed a passionate love affair with Earth's diversity. My experience of other cultures was my first exposure to the concept that different belief systems create different realities. The idea that our beliefs create our reality later formed the conceptual basis of the Empowerment Workshop.

I spent some time with the Peace Corps in West Africa. This experience awakened me to the way most of our world lives. It's an understatement to say that this way of living was a shock to my middle-class American mentality. Yet my African friends taught me not only about hardship. Their lives also taught me about joy, softness, sensuality, and the magic of simply being alive. I might never have found these spiritual gifts in our goal-oriented Western culture.

I left Africa by traversing the Sahara Desert by camel and truck. On the physical level it was a remarkable crossing, but it was also a symbolic crossing over to a new chapter of my life. I was scared and confused and had no idea of what was next for me, yet on that trip I met someone who introduced me to two practices that would become central to my life: meditation and therapy.

I began meditation training almost immediately upon returning to the United States. Sixteen years later, although I have had different teachers, studied various forms, and gone through ups and downs with my practice, meditation still remains precious to me. I find that my daily connection with the silence, or what I call "the mystery," nurtures, heals, and balances me in a way that is essential to my life.

In therapy I discovered that in order to become whole I had to uncover and heal the places where I hurt or was afraid. I learned that it took courage and patience to change unconscious parts of myself. I learned how hard I was on myself and what a joy it was to accept and love myself exactly the way I am. And, I might add, I'm still learning all of the above!

Through therapy I was introduced to the human potential movement, and what was at first an interest soon became a passion. I was fascinated by the field and I began to read books, take workshops, and find mentors. I studied gestalt, psychosynthesis, metaphysics, massage, and the Feldenkrais bodywork method. This eclectic approach taught me several things that found their way into the Empowerment Workshop. I became certain that, during the process of personal growth, the mental, emotional, physical, and spiritual levels of the human being must all be considered and integrated. Perhaps the most important thing I learned was that there is no one way to grow, that we each need to seek our own path to truth. The teachers who gave me the most didn't tell me what or how to believe, but rather encouraged me to look deeply inside and, above all, to stay awake.

As my inner development deepened I began to yearn for a way to express what I had been learning in meaningful action. During my university days I had been intensely involved with the antiwar activism of the time. Now, a decade later, the women's movement was sweeping America with a powerful message. I felt called to respond to that message and began working with different groups of women.

I found that people grew most easily in a loving, joyful, and playful environment. I discovered that many of the women I came across were in touch with their pain—and got stuck there. I discovered ways to help them heal the pain and build and implement new visions for their lives.

For the last seven years one particular group has been an instrumental part of my growth. This circle of women, called Helix, is a place where I can safely bring all of me, a place where I am healed and nourished. Among many things, these cherished friends have taught me that in order to give to others and the world at large, I must first love and care for myself.

In 1980 my personal growth took a quantum leap. I was in New York City leading a training session on play when an extremely attractive man named David caught my eye. One of my earliest memories with this man, who would turn out to be my husband and love of my life, was a passionate duel with the Styrofoam swords that we used for this part of the training. The play and dynamic tension of our co-creation started very early!

The journey of creating both marriage and life work as a team is not for the faint of heart. My partnership with David has been both the most challenging and the most rewarding learning experience of my life. We continue to teach each other the lessons of love, forgiveness, balance of power, honoring our differences, and how precious we are to one another. Our Empowerment work has been deeply enriched precisely because we are different.

For me, David, I was very fortunate to have had a loving and secure childhood with parents who gave me a lot of room to grow in my own way. They taught me to be open to new ideas and to seek my own path through life. I saw myself as an explorer of all that life had to offer. This exploration began to get exciting during my senior year of college in 1968. I had been studying international economics and realized that there had to be a lot more than this to life. Material well-being couldn't be the primary purpose for human existence. The Beatles were in their prime and venturing into the world of meditation and mysticism. I liked their music and decided to look into some of the other things they were doing. This was the start of my path to greater self-awareness. As I began experimenting with meditation, yoga, and Eastern thought, I found ideas and ways of being that were new and compelling.

After spending about nine or ten months practicing meditation and reading spiritual books, I found myself at a crossroads. The Eastern point of view was saying that the world was an illusion and the purpose of life was to transcend it through a higher state of consciousness. The Western material view held that one must learn to function effectively in the world in order to improve one's material existence. These two perspectives gave me a choice. It was the first point in my life at which I had to make a decision as to what I really thought. At twenty-one it was obvious that this decision would influence how I decided to spend the rest of my life. I chose to balance the two points of view and integrate a life of inner development with a life in the material world.

The next important step on my path was coming across a very obscure book on metaphysics. This book taught that your thoughts create what you experience in life. It gave the reader exercises to practice its principles. I followed them—and they worked. I knew I was discovering something important.

Over the next dozen years I read every book I could get my hands on that spoke about the art and science of affirmation and visualization. As I read and experimented with these principles and techniques, I realized I had come across a large part of my life's work—teaching people how to articulate and manifest a vision. I started teaching these ideas in businesses, educational settings, and open workshops. I also kept testing them in my life and refining my knowledge through personal experience.

As I was learning these universal principles and techniques, I continued to search for a spiritual dimension for my life. I wanted to learn more about meditation and how to connect with the deeper part of myself. I sought and found a spiritual teacher who helped me to develop spiritually and studied with him for a number of years. Eventually I learned what I needed to learn from him, and it was time to leave. His teaching style was to set up a dependency on him for spiritual guidance. I knew I needed to break away if I was to develop in my own right. And so I did.

At first I was confused by being on my own, because I had not developed my sense of self. Yet I realized that this was the starting place for me to find my own truth. I had to trust in my own ability to find what was right for me. Although I had self-confidence, spiritual knowledge, and the ability to meditate, I had never developed a sense of who I really was and what I really wanted. This was the next leg of my journey.

It took me through a number of human potential trainings. Through them I got in touch with the psychological and emotional side of my nature, which had not been addressed in the metaphysical and spiritual training I had done. I had previously been taught that you don't need to deal with this part of your nature, that meditation allows you to "transcend" your emotional and psychological issues. So I wound up either repressing or transcending quite a lot of my life. I was amazed to discover how much more there was to growth besides spiritual and metaphysical knowledge. I realized that my ability to use my metaphysical and spiritual knowledge effectively was very dependent on my psychological and emotional development. This realization formed the next major piece in my evolving understanding of personal growth and human potential.

As I continued to evolve I started feeling a need to integrate personal growth with social change. In my mid-twenties I became a board member of an organization called Planetary Citizens. The purpose of this organization was to help people recognize that all human beings are interdependent and we need to work together if we're going to deal with the many challenges the human family faces. Working with this organization was the beginning of a major commitment I was to make to positive change in the world. I had now found the final piece of the puzzle—a social context for my work.

Over the years I continually looked for ways to use the human potential knowledge I had gained to improve the world I live in. Along with designing human-potential training seminars for the general public and businesses, I applied this knowledge in inner-city ghettos and in helping minority business people become more successful as entrepreneurs. I found that my knowledge of the manifesting process was also invaluable in creating several large global-consciousness-raising events.

So as Gail and I talked on that special evening, my vision of empowering others was well set. I wanted to help people become self-reliant human beings, capable of realizing their dreams and experiencing their full human potential—physically, emotionally, mentally, spiritually, and as part of the whole world. The dance of partnership, comingling our learning experiences and our male and female perspectives, was about to begin.

In October of 1981 we conducted our first Empowerment Workshop in Boston. Since then the workshop has been our greatest teacher. It has taught us in an extraordinary way that although each of us is unique, we also share the bond of a common human condition. This has offered us the privilege of perspective and empathy toward our common humanity.

We dedicate this book to the thousands of Empowerment Workshop graduates who have enriched our lives and our teaching through the courage and nobility of spirit they demonstrated in stretching beyond their limits. And we offer this book to you, our reader, with the belief that it will help you develop your fullest potential as a human being.

Part One

Getting Ready

1

Introduction to Empowerment

Buckle up! You are about to go on an extraordinary life adventure. This adventure will call forth from you inner resources you may never have known you had. It will free you from boundaries that have limited you in the past and show you your power to shape your own destiny. On this journey you will learn the art of creating your life as you want it.

Most of us settle for far less in our lives than we are capable of achieving. We fall victim to impoverished dreams, dreams that don't begin to do justice to the potential we hold. We need to learn how to dream, how to boldly and courageously reach for our highest visions. This book will help you dare to dream *and*, equally important, give you the necessary skills and tools to realize these dreams. You will learn how to harness the passion of your heart and the power of your mind and create your fullest expression of being human. We call this empowerment.

On this journey of empowerment you will discover what it is you really want for and in your life. Discovering what you want is often a revelation in itself. Knowing your deepest heart can mean avoiding years spent pursuing other people's dreams. You will learn how to see and create a compelling vision of the life you truly desire.

Once you have a life vision worthy of your fullest effort, you will learn how to overcome those parts of yourself that can sabotage your intentions. You will learn techniques to remove disabling attitudes and bring your life vision into full manifestation. You will come away from this journey alive and capable in a way you never thought possible. Get ready for an adventure of a lifetime!

Watering the Seeds, Not the Weeds

Why is it that so few people are willing to dream boldly, to reach for their highest visions?

Part of the reason is that our culture is primarily pathologically based. It focuses on what is *wrong* with a person. Many therapies consider success to be helping people get "better," with "better" being defined as the absence of neurosis. There is rarely a direct focus on full potential or optimum well-being.

This is not a condemnation of these therapies; rather it is a sober look at our dominant cultural belief. This belief assumes a view of life in which each of us learns merely how to cope and fit in rather than to excel and move out. Much of the personal growth work that has evolved over the last twenty years reflects this dominant pathological attitude of our culture. This approach is rather like a gardener who spends so much time finding and pulling weeds that the planting, care, and cultivation of fruitful plants is ignored.

If you have gone through some of these therapies or growth experiences you will probably know why your life *doesn't* work—in great detail. You will have developed a theory as to what caused you to be the way you presently are and learned some tools for coping. This work is valuable and important in that it does help you cope more effectively with problems in your life.

However, it does not go far enough. Knowing that the reason you feel insecure is that your father withheld love from you when you were a child and learning how to accept this are just the first steps. Developing the self-love and inner resources to feel secure and confident throughout your life is another matter entirely, and you must learn the ways of this new world if you are to express your full potential.

We call this other world *creating vision for your life*. It is vital to direct our gaze away from our problems and inabilities. To create an inspired life vision we must develop an acute awareness of the possibilities that lie within us. Till we do this our potential remains dormant.

The empowerment growth process is so effective because it helps you to:

- Overcome the places in your life where you are having problems.
- Discover and manifest your fullest possibility as a human being.

The empowerment process teaches you how to release your creative energies and direct them toward achieving what you *really* want—from a healthier body to better relationships and sex; from material success to greater connection with your inner life.

You learn how to transform limiting beliefs and behavior patterns, how to overcome difficult life situations and problems, not as ends in themselves but as part of the process of self-creation. We refer to this shift as *moving from pathology to vision*. It is shifting our basic attitude toward life from problem-solving to vision-creating. For many of us this is a subtle and dramatic shift. It requires us to let go of the deep problem-oriented programming of our culture and accept the belief that we can and will create the life we want.

One person who went through this shift described it in the following way: "With the empowerment process I challenged myself to move away from the safe and familiar world of my problems. I developed the specific skills for exploring the risky, exciting, and positive frontier of creating what I want in my life."

Attaining this powerful a change in perspective is more than a simple overnight process. It takes time and requires us to be patient and compassionate with ourselves as we learn how to think and act in this compelling and dynamic new way.

Reasons for Your Journey

There are many reasons people choose to embark on this journey. The following list of reasons comes from people who have taken our Empowerment Workshop. See if you can identify with some of the goals described by others. Do any of these motivations ring true for you?

- I'm in a time of transition and I need to focus on what's next.
- I need to learn to deal with money.
- I need to take better care of myself.
- I want to attract a lasting relationship.
- I want to learn how to visualize; I've been hearing about it for years.
- I want to learn about me.
- I'm interested in the power of attitude and the changes it brings.
- I've got a lot of inner shoveling to do, and I need courage to do it.
- I wish to apply my personal growth interests in my workplace.
- I'm stuck in many areas of my life.
- I want to stop pulling the rug out from under myself whenever I get close to success.
- I want to learn how to focus on my goals and clarify what I want.
- I want to move away from concentrating on my problems.
- I have been asleep and it is time to wake up.
- I want to discover my spirituality.
- I have been too preoccupied with my work and want to find a way to be more balanced so I can discover the rest of my life.

Once a person has gone through the empowerment process, creative breakthroughs and dynamic self-growth begin to occur. The following stories come from people who took our Empowerment Workshop. They are examples of the kinds of challenges people confronted and the positive changes they brought about in their lives.

Janice had just ended yet another relationship. She felt devastated, sad, and alone. She had seen this pattern to her breakups before, and this time she felt as though she didn't have the energy to pick herself up and try again.

Through the empowerment process Janice began to examine her deep beliefs about loving herself and others. She slowly recognized how harshly she judged herself and how many beliefs she held about not being a worthy or good enough person. She realized how her own beliefs, conscious and unconscious, sabotaged both her ability to love and be loved. She learned more about her true self, not the self she thought she was supposed to be. She began the process of forgiving herself and others and building new life-affirming beliefs about herself.

When the workshop ended, Janice was clearer on both what she wanted from a relationship as well as what she had to offer. She was much more realistic about the hard work, commitment, and ongoing self-love required to make a relationship successful. Janice continued to use the empowerment process daily and attracted into her life a healthy, loving, and enduring relationship.

Lou came to the Empowerment Workshop with a prestigious job he had worked hard to achieve. He also had a good marriage and family life, yet he felt empty, something wasn't right. He felt as though his life was on automatic pilot and all the passion was gone. This confused him because it seemed like he had everything society said he needed to be happy. He said to himself, "I don't have the right to be unhappy." Yet he knew in his heart there was something essential missing.

With the same dedication he used to create success in his professional life, Lou dove into the empowerment process. With the help of the exercises, he reexamined his basic attitudes and premises about life. He looked closely at the life he had created for himself. He found that while he had devoted tremendous energy to taking care of his external life of family, home, and job, his internal life—feelings, reverence, wonder, spirit, and connection with the mystery of life—had been ignored. Lou was out of balance in a way that is highly typical of people in our culture. All the emphasis is put on the active state of "doing" while the receptive state of "being" is ignored.

With the assistance of the empowerment tools, he began to nourish his interior life. He created time with his family each week in which they could share their feelings and deeper thoughts with one another. He slowed down and spent more time with nature. Lou began learning the fine art of being: a soft, receptive state of mind in which he felt content in the moment without having to do or reach for more. After several months of genuine commitment to this new orientation, a profound shift took place. Lou felt more joy than he had ever remembered. He had a new verve for his job, more love to offer his family, and peace of mind. He had created balance between his outer and inner life.

Michael was an engineer with twenty years of experience in his field. Similar to Lou, Michael had a feeling of inertia, low energy, and a lack of joy in his life. Though their problems were similar, the empowerment process led Lou and Michael to very different destinations. It became clear to Michael that his career as an engineer no longer served him. Though engineering had originally been something he liked, it did not reflect who he was now. He recognized that by staying in his field of work he was numbing himself to experiencing life. He came to understand that if he wanted to feel energetic and enlivened again he needed to change his work.

Michael learned to clarify his current priorities and passions. He became aware that his real love was the outdoors. He discovered that he
wanted to find work outdoors that was meaningful to him and assisted
others in their growth. With patience, dedication to his new vision, and an
ongoing use of the empowerment tools, Michael did two things within the
next year. He left his engineering job, and he began working as an
Outward Bound instructor, leading men and women on wilderness vision
quests. He feels full of energy and impassioned by his new life work.

Fran grew up with a mother who regularly let her know that she wished
that she had never been born. Fran felt hurt, angry toward her mother,
and sorry for herself. She had also acquired a bad allergy at a young age,
which she felt was somehow connected to this situation. As she embarked
upon the empowerment journey Fran faced a double-edged challenge.
She needed to heal her relationship with her mother and overcome her
own cycle of feeling victimized.

She began examining her beliefs and attitudes and saw how they
had trapped her in the role of feeling helpless. Her web of beliefs looked
like this: To feel like she was a lovable person, her mother had to love
her. Since her mother's love for her was shaky at best, she had proof
that she was not a lovable person. If she wasn't lovable, she couldn't
love herself.

Fran became aware that the only way she could be free of her old
self-negating beliefs was to cut herself away from her past and start loving
herself. She succeeded. Fran even discovered that she could love her
mother while not condoning the way her mother had treated her. By the
end of these few months her acute allergy was gone.

Miracles DO Happen!

These stories represent people who felt a certain lack of well-being or
had a desire for more satisfaction in their lives. Can we call these stories
miracles? Yes—the kind of miracles that are available to any of us who
are willing to dream boldly, look honestly at ourselves, and commit to a
process of self-growth.

If someone told you that what you longed for in your life could be
yours, would you believe it? Before we used the methods we teach in this
book we might not have believed a claim like this. However, after years of
seeing the powerful results in our own lives and witnessing the remarkable achievements of others we've worked with, our answer to this question is an unqualified "Yes!"

The first questions that need to be answered on this adventure of
self-discovery and self-creation are: "Where am I going?" and "How will I
get there?" It's time to chart our course.

Planning Our Route

A Chinese proverb reads, "If you don't know where you are going, you won't know when you get there." An addendum to this is: Even if you do know where you are going, you can get there sooner and with less wear and tear if you know how to travel. The journey of self-discovery and self-creation is the most exciting, challenging, exhilarating, confounding journey you will ever take. It can be fraught with wrong turns and dead ends and has been known to be quite uncomfortable at times. It also has the potential to bring you happiness, peace of mind, joy, fulfillment, freedom, meaning, and enlightenment.

We invent all kinds of reasons to explain why we don't have what we want, but by and large they boil down to two: either

- We are not yet clear about what we want, or
- We have not yet learned the proper methods for creating it.

Throughout this book you will continually ask yourself the two questions at the heart of the experience we call empowerment: "What do I want?" "How do I create it?" The answers are what this book is dedicated to helping you achieve.

To answer these questions you will undertake a very special journey. Fortunately, you are not the first person to traverse this path. It has been navigated by many fellow travelers. And to assist you in reaping the most benefit from your travel, you will be accompanied by two seasoned personal guides: us. We will offer you insights gained from guiding many to their destinations.

John Steinbeck said, "We don't take a trip. A trip takes us." The person who returns from a true journey is never the same person as the one who departs. The returning traveler has new insight, new perspective, new richness of being. Life and self are seen with deeper wisdom and compassion.

We'll begin by giving you an overview of the inner adventures that lie in store. The journey of empowerment, like all trips, has three distinct stages: getting ready, traveling, and returning home. A successful trip requires proper preparation, a good itinerary, and a way to meaningfully integrate the experience into subsequent everyday life.

Getting Ready

- **Being in Shape** If you get yourself in shape prior to a journey, you can benefit from and enjoy it more. The first part of getting ready is to make sure you're well conditioned for the trip. On the empowerment journey, being in shape means both learning how to use your mind to create what you want for your life and developing the personal power to sustain your growth over time. With this preparation you will be in an excellent position to profit from your inner adventure.

• **Taking Stock** Before you leave on a long trip, it's important to take stock of important things and put them in order. The second part of your preparation involves taking stock of the way you view yourself and the world around you.

These views form your *core belief structure*. If these beliefs are healthy, you have the optimum environment for growth. If they are unhealthy, they can sabotage your ability to grow. As you take stock before your journey of empowerment, you will acquire the fundamental self-knowledge to build a healthy core belief structure. With this done you are ready to begin your travels.

Traveling

Your travel itinerary has seven legs, and this is where the action really starts. Each leg takes you deep into a vital aspect of your life, where you will work to discover and create what it is that you most desire. The seven legs you will travel are:

- Emotions
- Relationships
- Sexuality
- The body
- Money
- Work
- Spirituality

In each of these areas you will discover what it is you most deeply desire and learn how to bring it about. There are four steps to doing this:

1. Gather information to help you assess where you are and clarify what you want.
2. Construct a vision of what you want.
3. Clear any limiting beliefs in the way of your manifesting this vision.
4. Rework the vision: affirm, visualize, and energize it.

Returning Home

Each leg of your journey will be rich with learning, insight, and concrete knowledge you can use in your life right now. If you do the exercises. wholeheartedly, by the end of this inner adventure you will feel remarkably enlivened and empowered. This heightened well-being will testify to the commitment you have made to living your life fully. In this last stage, your return home, you will learn the most effective ways to sustain this heightened well-being over time.

How to Use This Book

This book is divided into three sections, which correspond to the above three stages of the journey. The chapters in each section contain concepts, principles, and ideas to help you discover your next level of growth in each area, as well as exercises and activities designed to bring that understanding into your everyday life. Each chapter builds sequentially on the knowledge and skills developed in the previous chapters, so it's important to follow the road map that's been developed for you. By following this map you will comprehensively cover all aspects of your life.

The exercises and techniques you will be working with are highly effective. They've been used with great success by the many people who have participated in our Empowerment Workshop. They will be successful for you, too, if you take the time to do them wholeheartedly. We get out of life what we put into it. What better investment can you make than taking the time to make your life all that you want it to be?

Many of the exercises ask you to respond by writing and, occasionally, drawing something. Expressing your responses on paper will help you immeasurably in gaining insight. You can either do this right in the book or use a personal journal to record your thoughts and observations. This journal will serve as a log of your inner travels and, as you will soon discover, become a very close companion to you on your journey. Many people like to get a special journal for this use.

We hope you will find this book useful at every stage of your growth. It was written to be used a second, third, or fourth time, as an integral part of your path to growth. Turn to it regularly and it will serve you well.

The Growing Edge: Your Spiritual Compass

Your experience of this journey is deeply connected with the way you view the growing process. Your attitude can either nourish and encourage your growth, allowing it to be a lively adventure, or undermine and sabotage it, making it an ordeal through which you nobly suffer. As you prepare for this journey of self-growth it's very important that you orient yourself properly. The notion of the *growing edge* will help you here. It will serve as a spiritual compass, aiding you in navigating the bends and turns that are part of the growing process.

The idea of the growing edge came to us as we observed the way things grow in the earth. A seed, planted in the ground, pushing up through the earth, overcoming whatever obstacles are in the way, first becoming a bud and then bursting into full bloom, is nothing short of a miracle. The new growth that has just pushed into the light of day for the first time is the plant's growing edge. It is that soft new edge of life that is just becoming.

This natural process contains a universal truth that applies equally well to human beings. Like nature, human beings who are vital and alive are always pushing out in new directions—they are growing. Those who are full of vitality are always thrusting out in new directions. The part of our being where this new growth is occurring is our growing edge. It's that place in who we are that is just coming into existence. *The growing edge is the point that our ever-evolving self is moving toward next.* Inherent in this growing edge are the steps we must take to create our life the way we want it, and on this journey, in each of the different parts of your life you will be discovering and cultivating your new edges.

While your growing edges may be different from those of someone else, there are a number of general growing edges that many of us have in common. The following are examples of one major growing edge from each area of life. Whether or not you are working with this particular edge, it will give you a sense of what we mean by this term.

Life Area	Growing Edge
Emotions	Getting in touch with true feelings and expressing them more freely
Relationships	Committing to more authentic and honest communication
Sexuality	Experiencing more caring and trust in lovemaking
The Body	Learning to love and care for it
Money	Believing that you can create greater prosperity
Work	Balancing the drive for success with a personal life
Spirituality	Developing a vital and personal spiritual path

While these examples give you a sense of several of the more common growing edges, they are just a small sampling of the wide variety of growing edges we human beings experience. Each growing edge will be experienced with any number of emotional textures, from joy to pain, from confusion to insight.

Sometimes there is fear of the unknown as you move to a new place within yourself. Just as often there is a deep sense of well-being as you learn to be more alive. Sometimes there is pain and discomfort as you move through a stuck or difficult place. At other times there is exhilaration as you break through a barrier. Whatever the feeling, you can be sure that *if you are on your growing edge you will feel energetically engaged in life.*

As the growing edge enlivens us it simultaneously frees us of the yoke of "shoulds" that weighs us down. We "should" be further along. We "should" be better than we are. Each of us is unique and has different growing edges. A tree doesn't judge and condemn itself if one of its branches is not as long as those of the tree next to it. One growing edge is not better or worse than another. It is just different. Understanding that growth is a *totally* individual process liberates us from that all-too-pervasive human foible of judging ourselves in relation to someone else or some preconceived notion of how we should be.

To grow is to be alive, and to be on the growing edge is to experience life in its most dynamic state, that of *becoming*. With an understanding of the growing edge you have a spiritual compass that will aid you well and with which you will become more skilled as your journey unfolds.

And now it is time for your first exploration of your growing edges!

Imagining Your Journey

Before you begin getting ready for the journey let's have some fun dreaming about it a little. Prior to a trip we love to pull out travel brochures, look at maps, and freely imagine what the journey might be like. Let's do some of that now. This exercise will stimulate your imagination and help you think creatively about areas of possible growth. You may come up with a preliminary itinerary of some places you will want to visit during the journey.

You will need a journal to do this exercise. (Some space has been left in case you don't have a journal.) As you answer each of the following questions see what comes to mind at the surface level and write that down. Then consider the question again and see if there is an answer that draws you deeper. Both the initial and subsequent responses are valid and will prove useful to you in your growth work. You may want to copy the questions into your journal so that you have them to refer to later.

Find a place to do the exercise where you will not be interrupted. Before you begin sit quietly and peacefully for a few moments to allow your mind to become calm and reflective.

EXERCISE

Exploring Your Growing Edges

1. What are the qualities within another that are most important to me in a relationship?

What qualities do I have to offer a relationship?

2. What is one thing I can do to create more love in my life?

More sensuality?

More passion?

3. If my body could speak to me, what would it tell me about how it's being treated?

4. If I had as much money as I wanted, what are the first five things I would do with it?

Why?

5. If I did not have to work for money what kind of work would I do?

Why?

6. Which emotion do I find most easy to express?

Why?

Which emotion do I find most difficult to express?

Why?

7. What are three things I can do to be more in touch with the wonder and mystery of life?

Bon Voyage!

2

Crafting Reality with Thought

We hope the questions posed at the end of the last chapter sparked your imagination and your excitement. It's time to get ready for your inner journey. You'll begin by learning how to more skillfully use the inherent creative power of our mind.

Of all the knowledge pertaining to the evolution of the human condition that has come to light in this extraordinary time in which we live, none is more promising than this idea: *We make and shape our character and the conditions of our life by what we think.* What you think and believe will manifest in your life. By becoming adept at intelligently *directing* your thought, you can become adept at creating the life that you want. You can take charge of your destiny.

You could spend years gathering self-knowledge and self-awareness, but in order to change anything you must be skillful in applying the principles of directed thought. Self-knowledge without skill in creating with thought renders your knowledge impotent. However, knowing how to create with thought without self-knowledge renders your life impotent. The empowerment growth process is uniquely designed to bring these two vital dimensions together: self-discovery and self-creation.

The in-depth approach we will be working with builds on any metaphysical training you already have but does not depend on any prior knowledge or experience. Indeed, for some people, prior knowledge has not been an asset. They learned an overly simplistic approach to creating with thought and became discouraged when it seemed ineffective. Others learned the skills, but without adequate self-knowledge they created things in their life that were not what they really wanted. Our approach to manifestation involves more than mastery of powerful techniques; it is mastery of a conscious, self-aware life.

The Principles of Manifestation

"And the night was still as they were given the greatest gift that humankind can receive—the formula for having their prayers answered."

—Anon

The formula we use has been around since the dawn of the universe. It is how the universe works. Every major practical philosophy has discovered these principles for manifestation, although often they shrouded them in mystical or religious-sounding language or kept them a secret.

Today this knowledge is readily available in language that is accessible to the average person. Because of its accessibility, people sometimes don't recognize the extraordinary power of these principles. We have been working with them for more than twenty years and are continually awed by them. As a matter of fact, it is only by working with these principles and techniques over a period of time that their extraordinary power can be clearly seen and appreciated.

As we learned how to skillfully apply the principles of thought, we discovered not only did we have the ability to have our prayers (otherwise known as affirmations and visualizations) answered but also that our lives took on greater grace and ease. We began living in harmony with the universe. The principles of manifestation and their application became clear, pragmatic guidelines for living our lives. This continues to be the most powerful knowledge we have, and we hold it with great respect.

We'll begin by laying out the three major principles of manifesting with thought so that you understand the *why*; then we'll lay out the techniques so that you understand the *how*. Often people learn the principles but don't know how to apply them, and just as often they learn the applications but don't know why they work. To be effective you need to know both.

There is no textbook to which one goes to find universal principles and the techniques that derive from them. What we will be sharing with you we have learned from our research, our own personal experience, and our observation and dialogue with the thousands of people with whom we have worked. You should find these ideas comprehensive and practical. Feel free to translate our ideas and language into any other tradition, metaphysical belief system, or way of viewing life with which you're comfortable. They all describe the operating principles of the same universe. Most important, use the principles and techniques in your life—and judge their usefulness for yourself.

The Principle of Creative Thought

Emerson said that what we think is what we create; he called this principle the "law of laws." Job stated, "Thou shall decree a thing and it shall be established unto thee." James Allen said, "The outer conditions of a person's life will always be found to reflect their inner beliefs." Seth said, "What exists physically exists first in thought and feeling. There is no other rule."

These are just a few of the many significant thinkers who pondered the nature of reality and came to understand the same principle: *Our thoughts and beliefs create everything that happens in our life.* What manifests in our life is a direct result of the thoughts that we are affirming.

What this means in practical terms is that the conditions and circumstances of our life at this very moment in time are directly a result of what we presently believe. If we want to change any part of our present life, we must first change those beliefs that created it. If we want to create anything new in our life, we must first mentally create the new belief. Nothing happens in our life without a preexisting belief that brings that thing to pass.

This sounds so simple at first. Why can't we all just affirm good things in our life and see them come to pass? If only the human condition were so simple! What makes the process complex is that *we are generally not aware of what we believe*. The vast majority of the beliefs that we are manifesting are unconscious, and unfortunately many of them are self-limiting.

We indiscriminately accept many limiting beliefs and never realize how much of an effect they are having on our lives. Thoughts like "I'm not good enough" or "I don't have what it takes to have (a loving relationship, prosperity, the work I want, peace of mind, etc.)" profoundly influence the shape of our individual worlds. Most of our pain, fear, and suffering are caused by these unconscious, unexamined, self-limiting beliefs.

To change these beliefs requires commitment, concentration, and courage to thoughtfully examine and alter the ways you view yourself and the world. The process of examining and transforming these limiting beliefs is what we call *mental clearing*.

The Principle of Mental Clearing

To be able to create the new we must first clear out the old. We can't effectively manifest a new belief if we are simultaneously holding on to an old, entrenched belief that opposes this new idea.

One of the major mistakes made by people working with the manifestation principles is to think that all that is required of them is to affirm what they want and it will happen. They don't realize they must first clear from their mind the self-limiting beliefs. *What manifests is what we* really *believe, not what we* would like *to believe*. Until our self-limiting beliefs are made conscious and transformed, they will continue to get in the way and inhibit our ability to create what we want.

Before we can create a belief that we have more financial abundance in our life, we must release our belief that there's not enough to go around. Before we can manifest a more loving attitude toward ourselves, we must first clear away any self-negating beliefs that say we're not good enough. Before we can learn any new spiritual ideas we must be willing to let go of our old ideas.

A story that illustrates this principle tells of a haughty Zen Buddhist scholar who goes to visit a Zen meditation master to learn how to meditate. The master invites the scholar in for tea, and immediately the scholar launches into a monologue on Zen philosophy.

The meditation master listens patiently for some time and then asks the scholar if he would like to have some tea. The scholar agrees and the meditation master begins to pour the tea into the scholar's cup. The cup fills up, yet the master continues to pour, and tea spills all over the table and the scholar. The scholar angrily asks what the teacher is doing. The master quietly replies that his cup was so full there was no room for the tea.

The master made the point that the scholar was so full of his own knowledge that there was no room for new learning. We must create space in order for the new to come in. Yet it is difficult to let go of the familiar. Even when parts of our present life are causing us pain and suffering, we often still won't let go. Our present discomfort is familiar and safe. It may represent our whole identity. So how do we let go?

There are specific techniques you will learn to use to dispel limiting beliefs throughout the rest of this book. A corollary principle to keep in mind, though, is that of:

The Principle of Vision

We are most willing to release old beliefs, emotional pain, and other baggage when we have a clear vision of what we will replace it with. The clearer the vision, the more we will be attracted to it, and the less we will need to hold on to self-limiting beliefs.

It's hard to get motivated to clear out the rocks, weeds, and stumps that presently exist on our plot of land without a vision of a garden. We need to see the new trapeze before we are willing to let go of the old one. We need to have a vision of the joy we will experience by loving before we will release the fear we have of being hurt. The principle of vision is: *In order to create anything you must have a vision of what it is you want to manifest. The more definite and clear the vision, the more definite and clear the manifestation.*

You are a sculptor molding an extraordinary, flexible, creative substance—thought. Your creation, which happens to be your life, will exactly embody the ideas and pictures you hold in your mind.

You may not know how you will get from here to there. In fact, you certainly won't know all the steps in between. But until you can envision the possibility, you will not begin to move toward it. Becoming clear about what you want your life to look like is not necessarily easy. Creating a vision for your life requires a willingness to explore and *discover what's important to you, not somebody else.* You need to ask yourself questions like: What do I value? What are my priorities? Where does my passion lie? What gives me meaning? What is my purpose in life? What is possible for me? This process has to be one of the most creative, dynamic, and demanding undertakings in which you will ever engage.

To the degree that you have a lucid personal vision in your mind, your life will begin to change in response to it. One of the most important things you will be doing on this journey is discovering and clearly articulating a clear vision for your life.

It is these three principles that explain the "why" of manifestation.

The Three Principles of Manifestation

- **The Principle of Creative Thought:** *What we believe is what we create.*

- **The Principle of Mental Clearing:** *We must clear our self-limiting beliefs before we can manifest new beliefs.*

- **The Principle of Vision:** *In order to manifest, we must have a clear vision of what we want to create.*

The Techniques of Manifestation

Let's now look at the "how" of manifestation—the techniques that allow us to apply these principles.

The process of manifesting our thoughts is the most natural thing we do. Whether we are aware of it or not we are always doing it. Our life today reflects what we've been thinking about in the past. Our life in the future will be a reflection of what we're thinking about now.

In other words, you are already manifesting, and the techniques you will be learning don't require any unusual ability. They do require that you be aware of where you want to direct your mental attention and that you learn how to do it with skill. They require that you be conscious of the manifesting process rather than continuing to unconsciously manifest things you don't want.

Think of your mind as a piece of fertile land. Taking control of your thoughts and beliefs makes the difference between a garden that you cultivate and a patch of earth that is left to grow wild. Whether cultivated or neglected, something will grow. If you don't plant the seeds of something you want to cultivate, then weeds will grow—and continue to produce more of the same.

There are two aspects to manifesting. First you need to create a potent mental seed, which consists of a directed thought called an *affirmation* and a specific image called a *visualization*. Then you need to cultivate and nourish this mental seed so that it grows to fruition—this is called the *energizing process*.

The Seed Thought:
AFFIRMATION

An affirmation is a statement affirming what you want in your life. It is an articulation of the new belief you are creating. To be effective it needs to be:

- **Written Down** The act of writing down an affirmation begins the process of making your intangible thought more concrete. You begin to experience the seed idea more sensually as you write it and see it. The process of putting a wish into sentence form demands that you be clear about what you want. There's a big difference between just thinking about something and actually writing it down. All of a sudden it moves out of daydreaming and fancy and begins to feel more real.

• **Stated in the Positive** Most of us have the tendency to approach growth as a process of overcoming problems as opposed to a process of creating something we want. We attempt to change something in our life that isn't working. This is generally done by negating what we don't want: "I'm no longer going to be afraid of my boss" or "I'm going to lose weight." The desired change can just as easily and with much greater power be stated in the positive: "I easily express myself with my boss" or "I am lean, healthy, and fit."

When we affirm what we don't want we are actually putting energy *into* it and nourishing it with our mental attention. Instead of getting rid of it we are bringing it more powerfully into our life. Going back to our example, every time we repeat the words "fear of my boss" and "being overweight" we reinforce the fear and the negative self-image and associate these unpleasant conditions with our life. We then have to apply mental energy to negate them. However, when you affirm positive thoughts, you immediately begin the process of manifesting the thing you desire.

One student of ours, after reframing his desire to quit smoking in the positive, wrote the following in his journal: "I did not smoke today and, for the most part, had no desire. I changed my focus from 'I should not smoke because it is bad for me' to 'I want to put only good things in my body.' This has made such a difference!"

• **Succinct** The more to the point and articulate your affirmation, the easier you can focus on it. A common mistake is combining several related issues into one statement. This weakens the power of the affirmation, for it is much easier to concentrate on one idea at a time than on several. If you find that you have combined two or more issues in one affirmation, all you need do is separate them into different statements.

Avoid making the affirmation wordy. You may tend to do this if you are not yet clear about what you want to create. The excess words result from this haziness. You may start by saying "I feel lousy whenever my boss talks to me that way. I know I could come back with a good reply if I weren't so afraid of him. I am failing to express everything that I am feeling, and that makes me feel worse. I know I could do so much better, and I resolve to do better in the future."

A positive, succinct affirmation that addresses the core of this issue would be "I easily express myself with my boss." An affirmation should not be an essay. It may start out as one, but it must be whittled down to the essentials if it is to carry power. It requires patience to keep paring away the words. But you are sculpting a single key thought. This key thought is the seed and not the whole tree!

• **Specific** If your affirmation is specific, you will be able to create clear results in your life. If it is fussy and vague, it will manifest fussy and vague results in your life. Many people walk around in a fog because they have been unwilling to take the time and make the commitment to be clear about what is important to them. They think life will somehow just work out even though they take little or no responsibility for making this happen.

Sometimes we look for reasons to avoid being specific. You may say "I can't be specific because I don't know what I want." If you don't know what you want, ask "What is important to me?" and focus on the specifics you do know. For example, if you want a new job, state all the details you do know and the date by which you want it. "I have a great new job that is rewarding and challenges me mentally in an outdoor environment; I'm making $35,000 a year by March 1."

Some people worry: "If I'm too specific, I may overlook something." The fact is that you'll never have all the information you need to make a decision. There will always be some information missing. Do the best you can, and if you find your first choice was not wise, learn from the experience and make a better choice next time. These sorts of "mistakes" will give you valuable feedback and are essential parts of the learning process. It is much better to move forward in this journey of self-discovery through trial and error than to sit still, never going anywhere for fear of taking the wrong first step.

Being specific is scary. It means committing to going for something important to you. It means that you may fail to achieve it. You may be disappointed, frustrated, and sad. You may create something that is not exactly what you want. You may make mistakes.

Stepping into the role of being the creator of your life is both challenging and exciting. When you start to get specific you realize just how much power you have. You realize that you are in charge of your own destiny. And the only way you become practiced at being a creator is through the act of creating. It's an evolutionary process, and your understanding of yourself and of the creative principles involved will evolve. There are no mistakes. What comes back to you is simply feedback that helps you refine your understanding of what you value in life.

Again, it's important to remember that you are creating your life every time you think a thought. The only difference is that now you are doing it with awareness.

• **Magnetic** Make your affirmation as attractive as possible. Use adjectives that you find exciting and enlivening. The language you use must represent your personal poetry. The more the language of the affirmation evokes deep feelings within you, the more you'll be able to put your full energy behind it.

Ready-made affirmations that you read in a book may be useful in helping you identify a growth issue but will generally not have personal enough language to engage your passion and life force.

For example, someone whose growing edge is his or her appearance might affirm "I am a nice-looking person who is always well dressed and attractive." While this is an accurate summary of their new belief, it can be stated in a much more enlivening way: "My appearance delights me and makes me proud to be alive!" The greater the passion in an affirmation, the more it will command your attention and belief.

- **Stated as if It Already Exists** The affirmation will manifest in the time frame that you create in your mind. If you want your seed thought to come to fruition now, you must state it in the present tense. If you state your affirmation as something that will happen in the future, it will always be in the future. "I am" or "I have" acknowledges that the mental seed is planted and can now grow. "I will" or "I hope" keeps the seed dormant as a future possibility. *We need to see the future in our mind as if it already exists. Don't worry for the moment about not knowing how you will get from here to there.* Remember, what we hold in our thoughts is what we create, whether or not we know the means by which the manifestation will happen.

- **Include You in It** Use "I," "me," your name, or any other method of allowing you to personally identify with the affirmation. Sometimes people make general statements such as "The universe is abundant," whereas what they are attempting to say is "I have an abundnt life."

If you are changing conditioning that came from others, it's helpful to state the affirmation in both the first and third person, saying "I am a lovable person" and "(My name) is a lovable person." This helps deepen your belief in the affirmation.

- **About Changes for Yourself, Not Others** Human nature being what it is, we often look at others as the cause of problems we might have with them, instead of looking at ourselves. With this point of view we say "If only my spouse, boss, mother, father would change, this problem would go away." It is the unusual person who says "I contributed to this problem and I can change it."

Other people use "God's will" as an excuse for not changing, saying, "It is God's will for me to be unhappy (or poor, or alone)." There is an adage to keep in mind if you find yourself using God to prevent yourself from growing: "God helps those who help themselves." Don't misuse the idea of "Let thy will be done" as a way of avoiding making decisions and clear choices in life.

The primary thing we do in fact always have control over is our attitude and behavior. If you direct your affirmations to bringing about changes in yourself, you will be surprised by how much this actually begins to affect your relationship with other people. As you change, the whole energy dynamic in the relationship changes. You may begin to perceive what seemed like the other person's "problem" as something that was caused by the particular way you both related to each other.

For instance, you could affirm, "My relationship is steady and wonderful as my husband learns to accept who I am." But this places responsibility squarely upon your husband and is a magnificent excuse for refusing to change yourself. We would suggest rephrasing this: "I have an unshakable ability, in all circumstances, to maintain a wonderful, caring relationship."

In order for someone to take advantage of another, someone has to play the role of the victim. If the person being victimized no longer chooses to be a victim, the person taking advantage must change. It's quite amazing to see how powerfully this works in practice. The most effective and enduring way to change a situation is to change yourself. (By the way, this doesn't rule out speaking to and working with the other person to resolve the problem.)

- **Kept on the Growing Edge to Avoid Sabotage** The affirmation must appear to be within the realm of possibility for you to accept it into your consciousness. If it is an unrealistically large stretch from where you are now, you will subconsciously throw up resistances. These resistances are limiting beliefs that have a lot of power for the simple reason that you believe them. That's why the affirmation can't be such a stretch that you sabotage it with resistance. However, it has to be enough of a stretch to excite you to want to create it.

If you have low self-esteem, you probably won't be able to believe an affirmation like "I love myself." This is too much of a stretch and you will in all likelihood subconsciously reject it. You need to back up a step or two and create an affirmation such as "I am capable of loving myself." After a while you may notice that you have grown and you are ready to tackle the affirmation "I love myself."

We build gradually. Our growing edges are the places where our sense of self is stretching to the limit. Our affirmations need to extend the boundaries of this sense of self without going so far out that they seem utterly impossible.

Creating an affirmation that addresses your growing edge is an art. This is the place where the insight you have gained from the psychological and spiritual self-awareness work you have done meets the skill you have attained in manifesting through affirmation and visualization. Together these approaches create the potential for lasting and fulfilling growth.

In summary, your affirmation should be:

- Written down.
- Stated in the positive.
- Succinct.
- Specific.
- Magnetic.

- Stated as if it already exists.
- One that includes you in it.
- About changes for yourself, not others.
- Kept on the growing edge.

The Seed Image:
VISUALIZATION

A visualization is a mental image or picture of what you want to create in your life. Some people find that they are more attracted to images than words because an image is more emotionally appealing. Others feel more comfortable working with the words of an affirmation because words can convey an idea more specifically. Affirmation and visualization used in tandem create the best results. Like a movie, images and narration together have the maximum impact.

Visualization does not require special skills that only visually oriented people have. It's a process of creativity and imagination rather than an optical technique.

In order to visualize, you need to think of an image that represents the thing that you want. If you want a house, begin to think about how you want that house to look. What style is it? Where is it located? How many rooms does it have? What is it made of? What colors is it painted?

If what you want is more intangible, such as more peace of mind, you can again build the image slowly, detail by detail. You can create an image of yourself as more peaceful. How does your face and body look when you are more serene? How do you physically move? *Voilà!* You have just sketched a mental picture.

Until you can visualize something as being possible, that thing cannot begin to manifest. You must see the possibility clearly in order to move toward it. The more clearly you can visualize what it is you want, the more easily you can manifest it.

If you can *think* of an image or picture, you are capable of manifesting it. Since everyone can think of images, everyone can manifest them. If you can see them clearly in your mind's eye, all the better. Once you have begun thinking in images, the vision of your mind's eye will improve.

To have the greatest power to manifest, your visualization should:

- **Evoke Feeling** Persuasive TV ads evoke feelings in us that make us want to buy the product. Your mental image should do the same thing. When you see your mental picture you should feel so excited that you want to bring it into your life immediately. The more emotionally appealing the picture, the more enthusiasm you will have to create it.

If, for example, you want to lose weight and become more fit, create an exciting mental image of your body the way you want it. Notice the details: the way a specific and *special* suit or outfit looks, what color it is, how it feels on, how healthy your body is, how proud you feel. Lo and behold, your emotion starts to build. It is this emotion and excitement that will be transferred into mental and physical actions and bring your visualized body image into real life.

- **Use a Single Image** Create a simple mental picture that is meaningful to you. It should be like a billboard depicting a highlight from a movie or a snapshot capturing a moment in time. If you tried to create a whole movie, your concentration would dissipate. If this billboard image is exciting enough to you, it will help evoke your desire to see the whole movie.

For example, if your goal is to have a romantic relationship, you may have many abstract ideas and random images of what that means. You may envision hurtling down a country lane together in a convertible, on your way to a wine tasting, or going on a skiing weekend, or dining by candlelight in a French restaurant.

This collection of ideas is not condensed enough to serve as a constant reference point for a powerful visualization. To develop a single image you should consider what is important to you in each of these thoughts. Abstract the *meaning* from each one by asking yourself what feeling you are seeking through each activity. Then find a single image that contains the meaning of each of the above, a single instant that embodies all these feelings. It might be, in the above example, the moment when, at a concert by your favorite singer, you touch hands and glance at your lover's eyes during the high point of your favorite song. Whatever the image, it should succinctly sum up all the meanings of that desire for you.

- **Include You in the Image** You are the leading star of this true-to-life story. Make sure you are in the billboard advertisement. See yourself happily enjoying whatever it is that you have mentally created. Allow yourself to feel the satisfaction and fulfillment of your accomplishment.

- **Be Literal or Metaphoric** Sometimes you will want to create an image that is an exact replication of something you want to bring into your life. At other times you may be more drawn to using metaphor. Which you do depends largely on how abstract the growth issue is that you are working on and on personal preference.

If you are working on developing greater personal prosperity, you might create a literal mental picture—you at a twenty-four-hour bank machine, having just punched in your code and staring at this enormous bank balance on the screen. If you are working on an attitude, say a belief in an abundant universe, you might create a metaphoric mental picture— you standing in a rapidly moving stream with the water flowing toward you easily and abundantly, or you standing in a beautiful natural setting breathing in the abundant invigorating air.

- **Be Physically Depicted** Like the affirmation, the act of expressing your visualization on paper begins to make it come alive physically. This has nothing to do with artistic ability. Stick figures and line drawings are totally satisfactory. You are the exclusive audience for this art show. You will discover, once you start, how much fun it is. The more fun it looks, the more attracted you will be to it and the sooner it can manifest. Be creative. Use colored pens and pastels to add more color to your drawing.

If you aren't inclined to draw, cut pictures from magazines, use photographs, or simply describe in words. The main thing is to do whatever allows the visualization to come alive for you. Also you might physically act out your visualization. This brings your visualization into your body and further enlivens it.

In summary, your visualization should:

- Evoke feeling.
- Use a single image.
- Include you in the image.
- Be literal or metaphoric.
- Be physically depicted.

Germination: The Energizing Process

A seed thought (affirmation) combined with a seed image (visualization) produces a mental seed (which is sometimes called a *thought form*). The affirmation and visualization process has literally given shape, definition, and form to a thought. This is now a potent, complete mental seed ready to grow. It now must be given the energy to germinate.

To allow your mental seed to grow and bloom, the first thing you need to do is create expectancy. You create whatever you expect to create. If you expect things to come your way, they come your way. If you expect things to be difficult for you, they are difficult. Henry Ford said it with elegant simplicity: "If you think you can, you can; if you think you can't, you can't." Our world is a picture of our expectations. What we *believe* we will have in our lives is what we *create* in our lives. To manifest your affirmation and visualization you need to believe it will manifest. You must have a confident expectation. You must have a state of knowing.

For some of your affirmations and visualizations, having this knowing is a breeze. As soon as you are clear about what you want, you know you will bring it about. In these instances the issue is about getting a clear vision, not about believing you can make the change.

Some changes, however, involve deep, long-standing, entrenched emotional patterns. The envisioned changes may seem insurmountable. How can you create belief in a new possibility when for so long you have not thought any change was possible?

You start by creating an affirmation and visualization that is on your growing edge, using the methods we've just described. The effort required to get to this point builds confidence and hope—an essential first step. You may not believe fully that your affirmation and visualization will manifest, but you believe that it is at least possible. Now you must nourish this seed and let nature take its course.

The principal way to nourish your affirmation and visualization is by the simple act of repeating and seeing it on a daily basis.

This constant attention slowly and ever so surely nourishes this mental seed, until one day you find yourself accepting this affirmation and visualization as a fact in your life: *You deeply believe it will manifest.* At this point you make the major shift from hoping to knowing, and the mental seed is germinated. Manifestation will begin.

On the pragmatic side you will start performing with a whole heart the actions that will assist manifestation. You are committed to a vision you believe will manifest, so you do what it takes to make it happen.

On the more intangible side you begin attracting to you the conditions, circumstances, and people necessary to bring your vision into manifestation. This latter aspect is a truly mysterious phenomenon. Just the right person all of a sudden appears in your life. Whatever you need seems to appear by "coincidence." In all the years we have experienced this process of mental attraction, we never cease to be awed by it.

Although this phenomenon is mysterious it is nonetheless perfectly reliable. For many years we had no satisfactory theory to explain how magnetic attraction worked. But the fact that we don't fully understand how something works doesn't stop us from being able to benefit from it.

Goethe describes it this way: "The moment one definitely commits oneself then Providence moves too. All sorts of things occur to help that would never otherwise have occurred. A whole stream of events issues from the decision, raising in one's favor all manner of unforeseen incidents, meetings, and material assistance, which no man would have dreamed would come his way."

It is the same magic that allows a seed you plant in the ground to attract what it needs to grow. Why this happens is part of the inexplicable mystery of the universe. The same principles that apply in the physical realm also apply in the more subtle mental realm. It is described well by the old Hermetic maxim, "As above, so below." *As soon as we believe in our vision we find ourselves attracting the worldly "nutrients" we need to have our mental seed grow to fruition.*

The principles and techniques outlined in this chapter will be put to regular use throughout your journey of empowerment. They will probably be trusted companions by the time you complete this journey. This is knowledge you can use for the rest of your life. You will have many opportunities to create and refine your unique affirmations and visualizations in subsequent chapters of this book. You will discover their power to create new possibilities for your life.

Many people have asked us the following questions as they began to use this new knowledge:

Questions on Creating Your Reality with Thought

QUESTION: How much time and effort do I need to put into my affirmation and visualization? Do I need to think about it all day long in order for it to manifest?

ANSWER: It is the *quality* of our mental attention, not the quantity, that counts. The key to having the mental seed you have created grow to fruition is your belief in it. You have to believe it will manifest.

This belief is not something that requires constant repetition throughout the day. As a matter of fact such repetition can be counterproductive, for underlying it is often the fear that your affirmation won't manifest. Remember, it is what we *really* believe that gets energized and manifested. If you spend just five minutes each day perhaps before you go to sleep, or when you wake up, or in the shower, or while exercising, and with full attention and knowing affirm and visualize what will be in your life, you've done it all.

It is also possible that you have created an affirmation and visualization that is so exciting that you can't help thinking about it. This is fine as long as it isn't done out of anxiety or fear. If we state our affirmation all day long because we're afraid it won't grow, if we keep digging up our mental seed to see if it is sprouting yet, we get in the way of a simple and natural process. Gentle knowing and patience seem to be qualities that most support the growing process. The patience of nature is a wonderful role model.

QUESTION: If my affirmation and visualization does not manifest, what does this mean?

ANSWER: It means that you need to look at the process you went through in conceiving it. Some of the questions you can ask yourself include:

• Am I on my growing edge? Am I so far out that my resistances will sabotage it? Am I so safe that I don't have enough incentive to create it?

• Have I been comprehensive enough in my mental clearing? Are there still uncleared, deeply held beliefs that run contrary to my affirmation? We will be discussing techniques for removing limiting beliefs in subsequent chapters.

• Is this something I really want to put my energy behind? Am I operating under someone else's belief? Have I the worldly skills to manifest this vision or do I need more knowledge? Is the climate in the world conducive to what I want to manifest? Or do I need to allow the seed to lay dormant for a while?

It is unusual that your first attempt will create your vision in the form that it will ultimately manifest. Your vision has to interact with the rest of the world—it needs to be seasoned with experience and practicality. For this to happen you must put your full intention behind your vision—and then *pay attention to what happens.* You will receive internal and external feedback. This knowledge is essential in helping you know if your vision is on course, enabling you to make adjustments to your vision. *If you don't recognize the process of feedback in manifesting your vision, you are overlooking an essential part of the way creation takes place.*

Manifesting a vision is not static and it is definitely not linear; rather it is an organic process of adapting and changing as we interact with many unknowns. A seed planted in the ground automatically adjusts as it interacts with rocks, roots, poor growing conditions, infertile soil, and so on. This is the way of growth and manifestation. It's no different for us. As we interact with the feedback we receive from inside ourselves and from others, we adjust our vision accordingly.

Beth spent some time attempting to manifest her vision and was unsuccessful. She thought she wanted to get married, yet none of the relationships she entered into lasted. She was about ready to consider herself a failure and give up hope at being able to create an enduring relationship with a man when she came to us.

After some exploration she discovered that her real passion wasn't in getting married. She was operating under her mother's belief, not hers. What she wanted was to experience life more fully before she settled into a long-term relationship.

Beth wasn't motivated strongly enough to energize her affirmation and visualization. It was someone else's dream that she had accepted unconsciously. When it came time to put her energy behind it, she discovered that it wasn't compelling for her. Beth's attention to the feedback she got (no relationship that lasted) allowed her to adjust her vision to what *she* wanted out of a relationship. She is now creating relationships without the pressure of them having to lead to marriage. She is much happier in these relationships as they are appropriate for where she is in her life.

Don't give up after the first try and say to yourself "I don't know how to do this" or "This doesn't work." Notice what happens and use the feedback as an opportunity for self-discovery. Learn from it and recraft your vision based on what you have learned.

The manifestation process will mirror your internal process perfectly; it can't be any other way. If you use the feedback you receive wisely, it will offer you the fruits of self-discovery and self-creation.

QUESTION: How does the idea of taking responsibility to create my own reality fit with the idea of going with the flow?

ANSWER: We can't avoid creating our reality; each time we think a thought we are creating it. Every belief we hold is shaping what we experience in our life. The process of noticing what we think and believe is the process of becoming conscious.

If by "going with the flow" you mean not making any choices or decisions and letting be what will be, then you are abnegating your ability to function as a conscious human being. You are using "being in the flow" as an excuse for being asleep at the wheel. You are deluding yourself. You are also misunderstanding the Taoist concept of being in the flow.

To be "in the flow" is to be in harmony with the universe. It is possible to come into active relationship with the universe and its ways. It requires conscious intention and skill to step into the flow. It's like getting on top of a wave and riding it. If you desire this way of being, you need to take responsibility for creating it. It won't just happen by itself. If you don't take responsibility for the sake of being "in the flow," your mind will become a collection of the unconscious beliefs you pick up as you float along. Like a twig on a river, you will constantly be getting bumped around.

The important thing to remember is that your thoughts are always creating your reality—*it's up to you to take charge of your thoughts and consciously create a reality that is fulfilling.* The alternative is a reality that is unconscious and haphazard. It's always your choice.

QUESTION: Am I responsible for creating *absolutely everything* that happens to me in my life?

ANSWER: If we accept the basic premise that our thoughts create our reality, it means that we need to take responsibility for creating all of our reality—the parts we like *and the parts we don't like.* Although it's easy to take responsibility for the good things, we would much rather find an outside source upon which to blame our misfortunes. For many of us it is scary to take total responsibility for our lives.

A large part of this fear comes from having to honestly look at our thinking and acknowledge that one or more of our beliefs were in error and the cause of our misfortune. Because our culture equates making an error with being bad, sinful, stupid, and unspiritual, our self-worth is threatened if we admit we made an error in our thinking.

As we broaden our understanding of the way growth takes place, we begin to recognize the difficult experiences we have in our life for what they truly are—*feedback about our beliefs.*

With this understanding we free ourselves of negative self-judgment. Our energy can now be freed up to create our new reality instead of being bound up in denying our old reality. We are now in a position to learn and grow from these experiences so we don't have to keep repeating them. Life becomes a living, evolving process in which we learn through trial and error; where *it's not only okay to make mistakes in our thinking, it's an inherent part of growing and being alive.*

QUESTION: Why do we hold beliefs that cause illness, accidents, or calamities?

ANSWER: Rarely does this occur from a consciously held desire. Until we are aware of our beliefs our experiences in life are created out of beliefs of which we're not conscious. *Most of us are so unaware of our beliefs that it is only by noticing the experiences we have in our life that we even know they exist.*

If we want to uncover the reason we are having a particular experience in our life, we need to ask ourselves this question: "What belief am I holding that is causing this experience to manifest?" If we're committed to peeling the layers of unconsciousness, we will find the belief and we'll help you on this one in subsequent chapters. Sometimes this belief will be muddled and at a subconscious level. Other times it will be something we say to ourselves all the time without ever pausing to recognize its impact.

A simple example is when we get sick. When we examine what we are thinking or unconsciously harboring, we may notice one of the following beliefs at play: "That (person, situation) makes me sick"; "I'm sick and tired of my job."

A subconscious belief might be "I need time to rest," or "I want to be cared for," or "I don't want to deal with my (work problem, domestic problem, spiritual problem)." There are many other variations on these themes.

This process of examining our beliefs is more complex when the situation we have created is traumatic or life-threatening. Anne, a participant in one of our workshops, had been in a serious automobile accident. For years she had blamed her physical disability on the driver of the car that had hit her. When she heard us saying that what we experience in our life is based on what we believe, she was incredulous. She said, "Forget this! I *didn't* cause myself to be in an automobile accident. I *didn't* desire to maim myself."

We didn't press the point, but we told her, that if she felt ready, it would be useful to examine what she was thinking about leading up to the accident. That night she barely slept as she lay in bed, tossing and turning, wondering if it were possible that her beliefs attracted this accident to her.

The next day Anne came into the workshop light and radiant. When she had gone back to that time in her life, she remembered that she had been feeling very depressed and angry at the tough breaks she had gotten in life. When she listened to what she kept telling herself, it sounded like "I am always the one getting hurt in life." She realized that she had an underlying belief that she was a victim and always got hurt.

When she discovered that the "accident" directly reflected her belief, she was astonished. She realized several things: "This 'thought creates reality' stuff is not hypothetical, but eminently relevant. If I can create bad things happening to me, I can create good as well! I can be as effective in creating new possibilities as I was adept at being victimized. It is time for me to release the anger I feel toward the other driver and God—and get on with my life!"

Since her insight and acceptance of what had happened, Anne has transformed her view of herself, from a victim to a creator of her own life. She began healing her body. Eventually she ran her first ten-kilometer race!

Anne didn't weigh herself down with blame or guilt for creating the accident. Rather, she honestly acknowledged the beliefs she was holding, accepted them for what they were, learned from them, and built her life from that point. She had a choice, and she chose to accept life as a learning and growing experience.

One last important thing: To account for an individual who is involved in a major calamity such as an earthquake, famine, war, or who has a birth defect, we must go to a subtler level to understand the cause. There are essentially two reasons: the choice of the soul before it incarnates to have a particular lesson or experience for its growth, and the coming to fruition of a belief held in a former lifetime (our beliefs create and are not limited by time).

Although this subject could be explored in far greater depth, it's not the purpose of this book. Our primary message is that you can create the life you want in your future by creating the beliefs that will bring it about. What you think now is what will determine your future, not what you thought in the past.

QUESTION: If, despite deep searching, I don't discover the belief that is causing me a difficult experience, can I change the experience?

ANSWER: For any number of reasons we may fall short as we attempt to find the belief at the root of a difficult experience. Sometimes it's because we need more self-awareness. Sometimes the belief is held at a very subtle level. Other times it's because we need more skill in using these metaphysical tools. And sometimes we're not willing to believe that we create our own reality.

Although this process is easier if we know what the belief was that caused the present situation, lack of that knowledge does not have to be a stumbling block. *Our power is in the present. If we are willing to take responsibility for what we are thinking now, we can change our future, regardless of what we thought in the past.*

Art had a life-threatening disease when he came to our workshop. He had a hard time accepting that he had created his condition, but he was willing to become more self-aware. Through the empowerment process he recognized the parts of his life-style and the mental attitudes that he needed to change.

With a total commitment he began noticing what he thought all day long. He recognized many unhealthy thought patterns. With the help of the mental clearing techniques he began to change them. He replaced these life-negating beliefs with more life-enhancing beliefs and *acted* on these new beliefs. He diligently employed his affirmations and visualizations, and in due course his health improved.

He healed himself by changing his present life-style and outlook on life. Although he had a difficult time taking responsibility for creating his disease, he *was* willing to take responsibility for his present and future.

What you're thinking right now is more important than what you've thought in the past. *The key to creating your future as you want it is your present thoughts and beliefs.* If you're unable to discern a past belief, or unwilling to fully accept the notion that your thoughts have created your present reality, fine. Build from right where you are. This very moment has all the power you need to create your future.

3

Personal Power

"Personal power decides who can and cannot profit by revelation."
—Don Juan

As you get ready for your journey you are gathering the skills and tools necessary for a successful trip. You now know how to create with thought. The next step is to develop the personal power to be able to sustain your growth over time. Personal power is what breathes life into our metaphysical knowledge and self-awareness. Without personal power we accumulate insight and knowledge, but nothing changes. The whole process is an intellectual exercise—interesting, but of no practical value. Many who want to grow and create more abundant and fulfilling lives fall short at this point on the journey. They read books, take workshops, and learn much, but they haven't developed the personal power to profit from what they have learned.

What is personal power? It is the ability to find your own individual truth and then create your life around this truth. It is finding the essence of yourself, validating it fully, and welcoming it into full expression. An *empowered person is one who has gone through the effort to find his or her truth and create a life vision around it and who is living this vision consistently over time.*

It takes time and effort to look at the limiting beliefs you have formed over a lifetime. These are the things that restrict personal power, that impede your fulfillment, that *disempower* you. And it takes personal power to transform those beliefs and create an evolving life vision that you sustain over a lifetime.

How do you acquire the personal power to bring this about? We'll start by looking at the seven qualities that make up personal power—we call them sources of power. Then we will lead you through several exercises that will help you cultivate or further develop these sources of power within yourself.

Finally, in the next chapter, we'll explore together those beliefs that either stand in the way of or fully support you as an empowered human being.

Sources of Personal Power

There are seven sources of power that we have found to be essential to creating and sustaining growth in life. Each of these seven can be thought of as a tool to help you cultivate and grow the mental seeds you create. You will feel adept at working with some of these sources of personal power, while others may be quite foreign to you. To have the capacity to sustain your growth over time, you need to develop all seven qualities within yourself.

To discover how you currently experience personal power, take a few minutes to answer these two questions in your journal or in the space provided.

1. What allows me to feel powerful in my life?

2. In what ways and in what situations do I not feel powerful?

In the first question you may have discovered that the primary way you feel powerful is by *doing* things in the world: exercising, making things happen in your work, taking charge of projects around the house, making money, getting ahead in your career. For you power is about asserting yourself in life, actively engaging in the process of creating.

Alternatively, you may have discovered that the primary way you feel powerful is by *being* in a certain way: being calm under pressure, demonstrating a sense of humor when things get difficult, being patient and understanding with another person, being in touch with and expressing your feelings, having an inner knowledge of the right thing to do. You experience power as your ability to receive the energy of a person or situation and respond appropriately to it.

Or you may have discovered that the primary way you feel powerful is in relationship to another person. It may either be to have *power over* another—managing another person, controlling the behavior of your child, telling your spouse what to do, having your point of view be dominant—or to *empower* another—helping another person to grow, learn, and become more powerful.

These are the *three primary ways we experience power: by doing, by being, and in relationship to others.* The first two make up personal power and when balanced allow us to have access to the full range of our power—our active, doing, masculine power along with our receptive, being, or feminine power. Standing alone, neither of these modes gives us sufficient power to sustain our growth. We need both. We need the active to get started, and we need the receptive to sustain us through the ups and downs of the growing process.

If the primary way you felt powerful was either over another or by empowering another this is important feedback. This is a false sense of power in that you are deriving it from interacting with another person. It is not coming from within yourself. When you are not interacting with another this form of power dissipates. And while it is obviously better to empower others than to control them, you're still not in touch with the source of power that springs from within you.

You probably had no problem thinking of ways that you do not feel powerful. This question helps many people pinpoint areas in their lives where they need to change, where they need to empower themselves. Many people feel powerless in some of the following areas: food, authority figures, emotions, sex, caring for their bodies, money, work, relationships . . . as a matter of fact, all the vital areas of life come up.

The seven sources of personal power that will help you sustain your personal growth over time are:

• **Commitment** Imagine that you have just made a breakthrough in the empowerment process. You have gained a wonderful insight into yourself and the changes you want to bring about. You've cleared away the mental weeds. You've created an affirmation and visualization that's right on your growing edge. You have a good understanding of how to nourish this affirmation on a daily basis.

What's needed now is the willingness to stay with your affirmation and visualization until it's manifested. The quality of personal power that enables this to happen is commitment.

Commitment is the willingness to stick with your vision throughout the inevitable ups and downs that occur. It is the active engagement of your full will and whole heart to carry your original intention through to fruition. It is the willingness to keep peeling back the layers of unconscious beliefs that come up in the form of your resistances.

Commitment requires much and gives back even more.

It gives us pride, the pride that comes from making good on our inner promises to ourselves.

It gives us confidence, the confidence that comes from seeing that we have what it takes to embody a vision.

It gives us satisfaction, the satisfaction that comes from stretching beyond ourselves and becoming more than we were before.

What is the key to developing commitment? It is having a compelling vision that attracts you irresistibly. You need a vision strong enough to sustain you when your energy and spirits flag. There is where the self-awareness you have embodied in your affirmations and visualizations is so valuable. It enables you to create a vision that you can believe in, a vision that is on your growing edge, a vision that so motivates and excites you that you're willing to stick with it through all the bumps on the ride.

• **Discipline** What happens after we commit to affirming and visualizing the vision we want to bring into our life? What can we do on a daily basis? We practice discipline.

We set up a time and a place to do our mental practice each morning or evening. In between these times, during the day, we stay aware. When old self-negating thoughts come into our mind, we do not allow them to hang around. We deliberately replace them with self-affirming thoughts.

Discipline is the hands-on aspect of commitment. It's the daily dedication to our vision. Discipline is very straightforward. It is rhythm with a clear purpose.

Discipline fails when we attempt to apply it without a compelling vision. Discipline for discipline's sake is pure drudgery. It is not sustainable over time. Athletic coaches, teachers, parents, and others have misunderstood this very important source of power. "Discipline" employed to build character, toughen, or punish is motivation through the negative. It will quite often, in the long run, produce the opposite of what is intended. Negating what you don't want energizes and manifests it. What we think about we create.

A compelling vision naturally brings about commitment. Commitment naturally brings about discipline. When our discipline starts to waver (as it will over time) we need to recommit to our vision. This brings life energy to our daily practice. *We need to keep remembering why we're doing what we're doing.* This is the secret of true discipline.

• **Support System** We may have an excellent sense of commitment and discipline, yet still find ourselves slacking off. To keep up our motivation we need something else. That something else is a personal growth support system.

A support system is comprised of friendships and relationships dedicated to helping us grow. A support system is a network of people whose priority is to both acknowledge our growth through love and affirmation *and* to give us honest feedback when we need a push.

A support system can include professionals (like a therapist or mentor) and close friends. It can include a women's group, a men's group, a couple's group, a twelve-step group, a therapy group, a spiritual organization, or something similar.

The critical factor in a support system is that the stated objective of the relationships involved is personal growth. There are many friendships and intimate relationships that are not explicitly intended to help us grow. These are fine. But we should not misunderstand the nature of such relationships.

You also need to recognize that some relationships actually hold back your growth. These people may be afraid of self-discovery, and this may prevent them from supporting your growth. Or their approach to growing may be dogmatic—they attempt to force their path on you. They may be self-destructive, and their negativity may close you down. If you have these kinds of influences in your environment, it's all the more important that you seek out a personal growth support system. It's also important that the non-supportive person be directly addressed and the situation changed.

It requires effort and a clear intention to seek out and build a support system. It often takes several attempts before you get what you want. Once you have a support system in place it requires a commitment to keep it alive and vital. It's so very easy to get caught up in the endless busyness of life and neglect your support system. Of course there may be a time when it's appropriate to let go of some aspect of your support system if it's no longer serving you and you've grown beyond it. You know whether or not you've outgrown it by asking yourself one simple question: Am I growing as a result of being in this group?

Another important kind of support is our physical environment. Our environments at home and at work are constantly affecting us. The colors, the type of art, the sense of order, the noises, and so forth are all influencing our internal state. We can create an environment that offers us calm, joy, inspiration, fun, or any other quality we feel will enhance our growth. However, to create our environment as a conscious part of our support system requires a clear intention.

Many people create a physical environment when they first move into a space—and never change it. The environment that they are interacting with, day after day, reflects who they were as a person many years ago. They have been growing but their environment has remained static.

With high-quality people and a physical support system, our growth can flourish.

- **Inner Guidance** How do we get answers to questions like "Is this support group helping me grow?" "What's my growing edge?" "What fears or limiting beliefs are blocking me?"

We get those answers from our inner guidance. Inner guidance has many names, depending on how it's being used. Some of these names include "intuition," "a hunch," "the still, small voice within," "our higher self," and "the wisdom within."

To become more aware of oneself, it is essential to draw answers from within. The more facile we are with this process, the easier our growth becomes. And it is easy—it's just a matter of doing it.

There are four steps that we have found helpful in accessing inner guidance:

1. *Get still.* We first need to turn off the mind chatter. This mental chatter is like the static on a radio—it disturbs our ability to hear anything significant. A few deep breaths can usually quiet the mind. If the issue you are attempting to receive inner guidance on is of a deeper nature,

several minutes of meditation on a calming image, such as a peaceful lake, will help.

2. *Ask.* If we want information, we need to ask for it; it doesn't just come. We need to turn on the radio if we want to hear music. The more clearly we ask the question, the clearer the answer we receive.

3. *Trust.* Many times people get very clear inner guidance but they discount it. They don't trust their own internal knowing. They don't believe in their intuition. They are totally bound in the rational mode of knowing. To prove its validity we must trust the inner guidance we get.

4. *Act.* When you receive inner guidance you must act on it. It doesn't do you any good to know something and not act on it. After you've followed your inner guidance, make a mental note of what happened. How did it turn out? As you experience concrete results from acting on your inner guidance, you begin to use it more. The more you use it, the more refined it gets and the better the results you achieve.

Inner guidance, a receptive source of personal power, is an important complement to the more active powers of commitment and discipline. It is like the fine focus on a binocular. A small correction is often the difference between seeing and not seeing or between a vision manifesting or languishing. Inner guidance provides the fine focus in our lives.

• **Lightness** Unless we approach our growth with a light spirit, we can easily lose perspective. Although we need to be serious about our growth if we want to change, we can't take ourselves too seriously. We need to walk our growth path with a light heart. The very center of the word *enlightenment* is the word *lighten*. As we grow we literally lighten. We shed the heaviness of limiting beliefs and emotional baggage that have weighed us down.

We all have different ways to create more lightness in our lives. Some people like to go dancing, others sing; some like to get together with the kinds of people with whom they have a good time. We have several couples we get together with for the sole purpose of having fun. We call our group the Space Rangers, and our motto is "The Space Rangers—dedicated to high adventure, play, and flights of magic." For each meeting we learn new jokes, create silly skits, or find new boogie music to dance to. Almost every time we get together our sides ache from laughing so hard at ourselves.

If we can keep our spirits light as we grow, it makes the whole process of growth a great deal easier. When was the last time you had a good belly laugh? Make sure you have a way to keep yourself light.

• **Love** To love ourselves, to love another, and to be loved by another all stimulate us to expand and open. It is in this state of loving openness that we are most capable of profound growth. For when we are in such a state our whole being is charged with love, and love is the most powerful motivating force in the universe. We are not approaching our growth out of "shoulds," or fear, or pain, or suffering. We are approaching it out of love.

The more we approach our growth as an act of self-love, the easier it becomes. It is fine for the impetus to grow to emerge out of loving and being loved by another, but we need to be careful not to set up a dependency on external love to motivate us. *The primary love relationship needs to be with the self.* We need to genuinely accept, validate, and nurture our selves each step along the way. It is vital that we regularly take time to appreciate and value ourselves for who we are now and who we're becoming. We need to wholeheartedly love ourselves.

The way to cultivate this love is to do just what you're doing—committing to self-discovery. As you open to deeper parts of yourself, the more in touch with your true nature you get and the more you discover its essence—love. It is this love that melts resistances, fears, and self-negation. It is this love that has compassion and patience for the human condition. It is this love that makes being human the special privilege and wonder that it is.

• **Finding Your Own Truth** This source of personal power is without doubt the most central to our definition of empowerment. *An empowered person has gone through the effort to find his or her own truth and is consistently over time living his or her life based on this truth.*

It is so easy to let someone else set up camp in our minds, to accept another's beliefs, to run our lives by another's values. Emerson, in his famous essay on self-reliance, says it well: "Nothing is at last sacred but the integrity of your own mind.... When private men shall act with original views, the luster will be transferred from the actions of kings to those of the individual."

Every one of us is a unique being with particular gifts, strengths, needs, lessons to learn, challenges to overcome, and contributions to make to the world. Our primary aspiration should be the discovery and creation of a life based on this composite of our uniqueness.

Yet it isn't easy to break out of the strong enculturation of expecting someone out there—the expert—to figure out the truth for us. We expect the doctor, the attorney, the newscaster, the politician, the priest, the guru, the therapist, to give us the answer. In our fast-food culture, we aren't encouraged to take the time to know who we are and what's important to us. We have become estranged from ourselves and one of our greatest sources of personal power—our unique inner truth.

Finding our own truth allows us to have a strong foundation upon which to build. It gives us core values and beliefs that we can use to evaluate our decisions. It gives us a solid identity from which we can develop a point of view. It gives us criteria for how we want to grow ... and much more.

Your own truth must be the guiding force for creating your life as you want it. And no one but you can create that truth. Almost every exercise in this book will assist you in discovering and creating your truth.

*   *   *

There you have it—seven precious sources of power that can help your growth immeasurably if you use them. It's now time to come into deeper rapport with each of these sources of personal power. The way we do this is through a process known as *guided visualization*.

We will guide you on an inner journey. All you need do is relax, come along for the ride, and notice the images and ideas that come to you. It is an effortless way to allow your beliefs and attitudes to emerge.

Approach this exercise with a fresh, childlike mind. There's nothing to figure out. It's like daydreaming. Just have fun and allow your imagination to roam freely. It's common to experience images, colors, or shapes, as well as words, thoughts, or feelings. You might experience nothing. After the exercise we'll help you understand and further consider what came to you.

EXERCISE

Personal Power Guided Visualization

Allow thirty minutes to do this exercise. You will need your journal and, if convenient, some colored pens, pencils, markers, crayons, or whatever for drawing images. Space has been left below in case you don't have your journal handy.

Find a quiet place where you will be undisturbed, sit in a comfortable chair, and, if handy, put on some soft, relaxing music. The guided visualization is divided into seven sections, one for each source of power. At certain points you will be guided to pause and close your eyes so you can more easily visualize and then draw or record in your journal what comes to you.

As you are writing or drawing in your journal, it will be helpful to keep your eyes half closed. We call this *soft eyes*; it allows you to move more easily back and forth between the imaginative and ordinary states of mind.

1. Imagine yourself walking through a brightly sunlit forest. You walk farther and farther into this sunlit forest until you come to a clearing. In the clearing you see a magical palace. You walk up to the palace, and as you enter through the main gateway you see many doors, each of a different color and shape. Pause for a moment to visualize this.

The first door you come to has "Commitment" written on it. Open this door and enter into the room of Commitment. In your imagination begin exploring the room of Commitment. What do you see—images, colors, or shapes? What do you hear—sounds, phrases, or words? And what do you feel—emotions, sensations?

Pause to explore this room for the next few minutes, then record in your journal the images, words, or feelings you discover. As you record your experiences in your journal keep your eyes soft as you move in and out of your imagination.

2. Now see yourself leaving the room of Commitment and closing the door behind you. You are back to the place in the palace with all the doors of different colors and shapes. This time you come to the door marked "Discipline." Open this door and enter into the room of Discipline. In your imagination begin to explore the room of Discipline. What do you see—images, colors, or shapes? What do you hear—sounds or words? And what do you feel?

Close your eyes and explore this room for the next few minutes. Then, with soft eyes, record in your journal the images, words, or feelings you discover.

3. Visualize yourself leaving the room of Discipline and closing the door behind you. Again you come back to the place in the palace where there are many doors of different colors and shapes. This time you come to the door marked "Support System." Open this door and enter the Support System room. In your imagination begin to explore the room. What do you see? What do you hear? What do you feel?

Close your eyes and explore this room for the next few minutes. Then, with soft eyes, record in your journal the images, words, or feelings you discover.

4. See yourself leaving the Support System room and closing the door behind you. Return to the place in the palace where there are many doors of different colors and shapes. This time you come to the door called "Inner Guidance." Open this door and enter the Inner Guidance room. What do you see, hear, and feel?

Close your eyes and explore this room for the next few minutes, then, with soft eyes, record in your journal any images, words, or feelings you have discovered in the room of Inner Guidance.

5. Leave the Inner Guidance room and close the door behind you. Again come back to the place in the palace where there are many doors. This time you come to the door of "Lightness." Open this door and enter the room of Lightness. What do you see, hear, and feel?

Close your eyes and explore this room for the next few minutes. Then, with soft eyes, record in your journal images, words, or feelings you discover.

6. See yourself leaving the room of Lightness and closing the door behind you. Find yourself back at the place in the palace where there are many doors of different colors and shapes. This time you choose the door called "Love."

You open this door and enter the room of Love. What do you see, hear, and feel? Close your eyes and explore this room for the next few minutes, and then, with soft eyes, record in your journal images, words, or feelings you discover.

7. Leave the room of Love and close the door behind you. You are back at the place in the palace where there are many doors of different colors and shapes. This time you approach the final door, the door marked "Finding Your Own Truth." Open this door and enter the room of Finding Your Own Truth. What do you see—images, colors, or shapes? What do you hear—sounds, phrases, or words? And what do you feel—emotions, sensations?

In your imagination explore this room for the next few minutes and with soft eyes record in your journal images, words, or feelings you discover.

See yourself leaving the room of Find Your Own Truth and closing the door behind you. It's now time to come back. Imagine yourself passing by all the different doors and pondering your discoveries: Love, Lightness, Inner Guidance, Support System, Discipline, Commitment. Pause.

Go back through the main gateway through which you entered the palace. Enter the forest and begin walking out. Proceed nearer and nearer to the edge of the forest. Finally, come out of the forest. You are back, fully alert, and fully here and now.

Interpreting and Learning from Your Visualization

We hope you have enjoyed this exercise. You now may be asking yourself, "What do I make of what I discovered in the different rooms?" Some people do lots of drawing and others lots of writing. Some get information in a symbolic way, others in a more literal way. Some don't see or hear anything; they just get feelings. What's important to know about guided visualization is that there is no one way it's supposed to be.

Each of us is different. Each of us accesses the subconscious mind in our own way.

As you look over what you entered in your journal, for each source of power ask yourself, "Does this suggest that I have a healthy relationship or an unhealthy relationship with this quality?" Where you find a healthy relationship to a source of personal power, notice it. Acknowledge and affirm this strength. Draw on this quality as a real asset in your growing process. Where you find an unhealthy relationship, appreciate yourself for becoming aware of it. That's the first step in any growing you do. Once we're aware of something we can begin to make changes.

Let's look at how to make changes through seeing how other people used the information they received from this exercise.

When Judith went into her Support System room she had a feeling of fullness and aliveness. The room was filled with people who cared for her. Her boss was smiling, and her family rushed to hug her. Other close friends in the background were waving and releasing balloons with personal messages of how wonderful they thought she was.

She wrote in her journal, "I realize that I am deeply supported in my life. People value me and are there for me when I need them. I feel very fortunate in this part of my life." For Judith her support system was a real strength she could draw upon.

Jean had this to say: "In the room of Support System, I found myself suspended on pipes, as if I were being held up by a lot of different poles. They were sticking me up quite high, so my feet didn't touch the ground. I was supported but I couldn't go anywhere. This helped me recognize the fact that, in my life, the people around me aren't really helpful in understanding who I am and what my personal work has to be. I realized that I have to get out on my own. I must redo this room."

Marcia had great difficulty even opening the door to the Support System room. When she finally got in the room it was very blurry and she had only a vague sense of shadowy figures in the corners. Marcia felt uneasy and empty in this room. Marcia wrote in her journal, "I feel the images reflect the way I isolate myself from other people. I'm afraid of getting close to people, it's too scary for me. I don't have support because I'm afraid of intimacy."

Understanding the importance of nonjudgmental feedback, Marcia did not judge or blame herself. She saw the information as input. How did she work with this input? To begin with, she was compassionate with herself. She acknowledged that this was a growing edge for her. She did not put herself in the wrong because she didn't have a support system. Instead she began using an empowerment tool that was created specifically for this exercise—becoming an interior designer and redecorating her room.

Being Your Own Interior Designer

In all likelihood you found some rooms you were pleased with or even excited by and some rooms you didn't care for at all. You may even have had a room in which you saw nothing. These experiences were your personal feedback about your current relationship with each aspect of your personal power. This kind of self-awareness is the first step. The next exercise will help you redecorate each room the way you want it. As you change your mental images of what is present in that room, you set the stage for those changes to occur in your life.

The redecorating process is an easy and fun way to enhance your relationship to a source of personal power. Marcia began visualizing her room with distinct, clear images of specific people who were on a path of growth. She saw herself interacting with these people and enjoying it. She visualized herself putting up pink wallpaper with hearts. She added lots of flowers and plenty of windows with the sun shining in. She arranged the furniture so that she could talk with others more intimately. As her own interior decorator she designed her room exactly as she needed it to help with this growing edge.

Charlie's lightness room also had no floor! He gulped and acknowledged that his life, inwardly and outwardly, was indeed much too serious. So he completely redecorated this room. First he put in a rainbow-colored floor. He put every fun person he had ever known in his room. He took his favorite comedians and had them offering private joke sessions just for him. He played zany games with his kids. Everybody in his room was laughing.

Each day Charlie went to his lightness room as part of his meditation, and after about two weeks of doing this a shift took place. Charlie noticed himself lightening up. He no longer felt he needed to work until eight each night. He found that he could make time to play with his kids and that it was actually fun. He discovered a new treat—taking his wife out dancing. He even started looking forward to his meditation each day, since he was now meditating on lightness. Meditation started becoming fun, as opposed to another obligation he went through to become spiritual. Charlie began enjoying his life in a way he never thought possible.

EXERCISE

Redesigning Your Rooms

1. Think back over your rooms of personal power and see which ones need to be redesigned. You may decide some rooms are perfect the way they are, some rooms may require only new paint or wallpaper, while others may require a major overhaul. Check off on this list those rooms that need redesigning.

- Commitment
- Inner Guidance
- Discipline
- Support System
- Lightness
- Love
- Finding Your Own Truth

2. Use your creativity and imagination to design the interior of each, one at a time, exactly as you wish it to be. Describe each new design here.

3. Spend a few minutes simply enjoying the changes you have made in each room. Soak up the experience of how it feels to spend time in each self-created room.

4. Spend a few minutes each day visiting the new rooms of your palace and soaking up these wonderful new experiences. You'll be amazed by the positive changes that begin to occur. Who said growing couldn't be fun?

4

Core Beliefs

Now that you have an understanding of how to create with thought and your personal power is revved up, you're in good shape for the journey. The final act of getting ready is to take stock and put things in order. Specifically, this means creating the healthiest view you can of yourself and your world—putting your core beliefs in order.

How much do you really know about yourself? Have you ever actually taken time to consider who you are apart from your work, your family, or your interests? Why do you believe what you do about yourself? Why do you believe what you do about the world? Have you ever wondered how you came to formulate these opinions?

The ideas you hold about yourself and the world around you make up your core beliefs. For the most part these core beliefs are unconscious and unexamined. What makes these beliefs so important is that almost every action you take in your life is influenced by them. If you want to be in charge of your life, you must examine and understand the beliefs that are causing you to act the way you do *and* change those beliefs that are not serving you.

Mental Programming

Much of our basic mental programming comes in our childhood. We are most influenced by the beliefs our parents hold and communicate to us through their words and actions. Our beliefs are also shaped by teachers, religion, siblings, and other close family members, classmates, community, country, and life experiences in general.

As children we have not developed filters that allow us to discriminate between helpful and unhelpful beliefs. Those early direct and indirect statements about ourselves and about the world penetrate deeply into our psyche. As children we uncritically accept what we are told and shown as fundamental truths, and we rarely question these "truths" in later life. Most of our actions today are determined by the core beliefs we took on at a young age.

Although this early mental programming has the most pervasive influence on our actions, our core belief structure is continuously being re-shaped by co-workers, family, media, authority figures, our particular subcultures, and more. Considering we live in an unenlightened world, it is to be expected that we have acquired negative programming.

Discovering Your Core Beliefs

How do you discover which beliefs are core? A core belief is one that is so basic to the way you orient yourself in your life *that you never stop to think about it*. You simply take this belief for granted and operate from it automatically. You are so sure that "This is just who I am and the way I think" that you never stop to consider that there is a deeply held belief causing you to think the way you do. These beliefs may not influence the *details* of each decision you make during the day, but they certainly influence the *tone* of these decisions and the overall direction they drive you in. These beliefs are fundamental to the way you orient your life.

Working with many people has led us to identify five general areas in which most people hold core beliefs—fundamentally affecting their thoughts and actions. Although there may be more, the major personal growth issues that people face stem from these five categories of core beliefs. Because they are so much a part of our lives, all of us have a relationship to these beliefs, albeit in most cases unconscious.

These core beliefs are like the soil in a garden. If the soil is fertile you can plant seeds in it and they will grow, but if the soil is infertile you can have the very best seeds and they still won't grow. As we've said, the dreams and visions you want in your life are the mental seeds you plant on this journey. The critical work ahead of you in this chapter is cultivating your mental soil—your core belief system—so that it is fertile for growth, not filled with rocks and weeds. With this done, you can be assured of a successful journey.

We'll begin by describing the five categories of core beliefs and then afterward invite you to do an inner soil check to determine where you need to weed out or fertilize your mental garden. As the beliefs are described you may find yourself being self-critical—"shoulding" on yourself. If this happens, remember that these beliefs are so basic to our experience of being human that they can be considered the core earth curriculum. Everyone on earth works on them at some level or other. If you haven't mastered them yet, be patient—you're on the right planet!

- **Self-responsibility** When something doesn't work out the way you want it to, what do you say to yourself? When a misfortune occurs in your life, how do you respond? When someone does something to you that you don't like, what do you think to yourself?

One internal dialogue might be: "Why does this always have to happen to me? I seem to have the worst luck. He screwed me. I wish my life were like so-and-so's, then things would be so much better," and endless variations on this theme.

Taking this stance, we feel victimized by a life experience and, to a greater or lesser degree, immobilized. We are unwilling to take responsibility for the experience. We attempt to place blame on something or someone outside of ourselves. We become a victim.

Another internal dialogue might be: "I feel terrible, and it hurts. What can I learn from this experience? Let me pick up the pieces, learn what I can, and I'll be a better person for this" . . . and variations on this theme.

When we take this stance we make a different choice. We accept what has happened. We don't deny the pain or sadness, yet at the same time we attempt to learn, grow, and profit from the experience. *We take responsibility for our experience.* One stance is life-negating, the other, life-affirming. We always *have a choice as to how we are going to respond to any life experience.*

Looking at this category of core beliefs from a broader point of view, imagine life as a big classroom where we each come to learn different lessons that help us evolve as human beings. Some of the classes are fun and joyful, some are extremely challenging and downright painful.

Yet, if we have a class in our life, it's for a reason. We need to take responsibility to attend it and learn the lessons it has to teach us. If we continually confront ourselves with the same lessons, we tread an endless round of boring repetition. But if we learn the lesson, we graduate! Once we've graduated we aren't doomed to repeat the lesson. Even if it comes up again, we have attained mastery and it is handled easily.

• **Self-esteem** Do you feel that you are a lovable person? Do you feel confident in your abilities? Do you believe you have what it takes to be successful in all the areas of your life? Do you believe you are worthy of a happy and abundant life?

Most of us grow up with people criticizing us; this negatively affects how we feel about ourselves. Grades, physical appearance, intelligence, athletic prowess, and social skills are some of the more common places where we get negated. These criticisms often damage our young and fragile egos. If we are not affirmed, loved, accepted for who we are, and taught how to develop our abilities, we are going to have self-esteem issues to sort out as an adult. Since many of us have not had consistently positive upbringings, we often find areas in our life where we have a negative self-image when we look honestly at ourselves.

You may discover that you have high self-esteem in your work, but in relationships you feel like a flop. You may feel wonderful about your spirituality but lousy about your body. You may take pleasure in yourself as a lover but put yourself down because you can't earn enough money. If you have any of these self-negating attitudes and you don't change them, they will undermine you in those areas of your life.

Welcome to the human condition!

• **Trust in the Universe** Do you believe you are part of a larger universe that is supportive and benevolent? Do you believe that there is a higher intelligence in the universe that cares for your well-being and to which you can go in times of need? How you answer these questions has a powerful influence on how you orient your life.

People who trust the universe feel supported in life and act with a sense of security. They are willing to take more risks because they feel part of the very breath of life. They know that if they fall they will be caught by the universe itself. They are not gripped by fear, and this gives them a feeling of inner peace. This larger context for their lives allows these people to feel buoyant.

For those who don't trust the universe the picture is quite different. They're in life totally by themselves. Because they consider the universe untrustworthy, they must continually protect themselves against those who might take advantage of them. They move through life with caution, fear, and inner loneliness. They don't feel supported.

Some of us have this trust, some of us don't. It has nothing to do with whether we've read spiritual books or are loving people. It transcends ideas and even the kindest heart. It is out of the domain of religious teachings, which attempt to tell people which way they should think about the universe or God. You can't be told to trust; it comes from a place deep inside. However, you can cultivate or deepen this attitude of trust if you desire, for it is like any other belief—available to anyone who wants it.

- **Positive Attitude** Do you look at a half-filled glass of water and perceive it as being half full or half empty? Do you see life as a problem to be overcome or an opportunity to be experienced? When something difficult happens to you is your first response to look for the positive or the negative in that situation?

A positive attitude is not about putting your head in the sand and attempting to say everything is okay when it isn't. It is not having the Pollyanna belief that everything is okay when it is obviously not. A *positive attitude means looking reality straight in the eye and seeing what can be constructively created from each situation you encounter.* It requires courage and strength of mind to unflinchingly face the truth and, amid the many paradoxes of life, find the good, the valuable, the noble.

Unfortunately most people have found it too difficult to hold a positive charge in the face of today's world. They have found it easier to give in and give up. Even more sad, many people in the name of being sophisticated have fallen victim to a major mental disease of our time—cynicism. For them nothing ever has to work. They affirm the least developed aspects of people and institutions. They have bought a house at the bottom of the mountain.

Perhaps the best argument for having a positive attitude is a very practical one. Metaphysical writer Richard Keiniger writes, "To have a positive mental attitude gives rise to undaunted living. To fear calamity brings one to see only the gloomy aspects of everything, and lo and behold, calamity dogs at one's heels. Bargain with life for a penny and no more than a penny will be acquired. If you unwaveringly believe and expect life to bring you love, health, and prosperity, then these blessings shall become manifest in your life; for such as the power of mental energy over the physical plane of existence. A positive attitude when one consciously uses it becomes a practical tool."

- **Flowing with Change** Do you get upset when something unexpected occurs? Are you anxious when circumstances change and you can't control them? Do you have a "Plan B" ready just in case?

Most of us in this culture have grown up believing that life is about being secure and stable. We build our actions on this belief and work very hard to create security in our life. When changes occur we are unprepared and we become anxious and stressed. We become stressed because we are building our reality on an illusion—the illusion that stability is a natural law.

The nature of the universe is to change. This applies to all its inhabitants, large and small. As much as we would like things to remain the way they are, it just isn't the way things work here. Things are always changing—they grow, evolve, break down, and transform into something new.

Seeking a security based on things remaining the way they are is even more misguided today than it was in the past. Our society is changing more rapidly than ever before. Many of our major social assumptions are being challenged. We are living in a society in metamorphosis. Those that can't adapt in this time of rapid change are at risk of being left behind, clinging to outmoded ideas that are crumbling and falling ill with stress-related diseases.

Life is a moving river and we must learn how to flow with it. There is no one way to do this. Each of us must find his or her own way. Some of those ways are spiritual, others are material, and still others are emotional. Some people actually enjoy this change process so much that they seek out white water for greater challenge and excitement. Others are content to just avoid crashing into boulders. Whichever approach you take, *it is smart to become comfortable with change, because we are heading for more of it, not less.*

How healthy are your core beliefs? It's quite normal to be holding core beliefs that need some plowing and tilling. If you're on this planet, you can't help but be affected by the beliefs of those around you. Everybody picks up negative programming—it's part and parcel of being human. But we don't have to keep those core beliefs that make our mental soil infertile for growing and sabotage the new mental seeds we try to plant. Fertilizing your core beliefs—your mental soil—is essential to the next stage of your growing process.

Tilling Your Inner Soil

It is now time to examine the quality of your mental soil to determine which nutrients or fertilizer need to be added. The richer the inner soil, the easier it will be for the mental seeds you are planting to grow. The following exercise examines your core belief structure. It brings some of those dusty subconscious beliefs out into the light where you can examine and deal with them. In this chapter you begin the process of making changes based on your conscious choices of how you would like your life to be.

Although each person has his or her own unique issues to work through, we have found that there are a number of growing edges that many people have in common. Consider the lists below and check off any statements in them that represent your growing edge. Check off more than one if applicable. Then, using these examples to start you thinking, write down your response in more detail to the questions that follow.

For your answers to be most useful to you, try to think of responses for each of the seven vital life areas. If you don't have responses for some of the life areas, then just skip over them. They are:

- Emotions
- Relationships
- Sexuality
- Money
- Work
- The body
- Spirituality

EXERCISE

Inner Soil Test

- **SELF-RESPONSIBILITY**

  Common Growing-Edge Issues

  - I'm a victim to forces beyond my control.
  - I don't have the power to change my life.
  - I am helpless.
  - I don't know how to deal with difficult things.
  - I stay confused so I don't have to take responsibility for my life.
  - I can't change my life, I've got bad karma.
  - It's my parents' fault that my life is messed up.
  - So-and-so did it to me.
  - I'm always the one who gets the raw end of the deal.
  - I don't know how to change and grow.

Now ask yourself: How willing am I to take responsibility for the experiences, both easy and difficult, that I have in my life? Explain how this plays out in daily life. What can I do to take more responsibility for my life?

- **SELF-ESTEEM**

  Common Growing-Edge Issues

  - I'm not good enough.
  - I don't have what it takes to be successful.
  - I'm not lovable.
  - I'm not worthy.
  - I don't deserve prosperity, a loving relationship, health, etc.
  - I'm not smart enough.
  - I don't like myself.
  - I don't accept myself.
  - I don't approve of myself.
  - I'm not capable.

  Ask yourself: How much do I believe in myself? How is this apparent in my daily life? What can I do to believe in myself more?

- **TRUSTING THE UNIVERSE**

  Common Growing-Edge Issues

  - I'm all alone in my life.
  - I don't believe that there is a benevolent being or universe.
  - I can't let go.
  - I can't give up control to something larger than myself.
  - If I don't constantly look out for myself, I will be taken advantage of.
  - If I trust the universe, I will be hurt.
  - People will rip you off if you give them a chance.
  - I don't know how to trust.
  - There is no intelligent universe.

  Ask yourself: How much do I believe the universe (i.e., the larger environment, God, universal intelligence, the life force, or whatever words you choose) supports me? How does this affect my daily life? What can I do to develop more trust in a supportive universe?

• POSITIVE ATTITUDE

Common Growing-Edge Issues

- Life is hard.
- Life is a struggle.
- My fate in life is to suffer.
- The world is a corrupt place.
- Nothing I do makes a difference.
- Something bad always happens to me.
- There's always something.
- The world is a mess.
- Corporations, government, politicians, etc., are bad.
- It'll never work.
- It can't be done.
- I knew this would happen.
- I never succeed in life.

Ask yourself: Is my mental attitude toward life mostly positive or mostly negative? How is this apparent in my daily life? How can I cultivate a more positive mental attitude?

• FLOWING WITH CHANGE

Common Growing-Edge Issues

- Unexpected changes will overwhelm me, I won't know what to do.
- I need to have security to feel safe in my life.

- I'm afraid change will hurt me.
- What I can't control won't turn out right.
- Change is too painful and difficult, I'd rather keep things the same.
- I don't have the willpower to sustain any changes.

Ask yourself: In what areas of my life do I find it the most difficult to flow with change? How can I accept and flow with change more easily?

Nourishing Your Inner Soil

The information you gained from the inner soil test should have given you a good sense of how you view yourself and the world around you. Here are some of the insights other people have gained:

Amanda had the following experience of self-esteem: "I wrote down that 'Knowing myself is more appropriate than believing things.' To the degree that I am conscious of who I am, I bring this self-awareness to play and work and it continually unfolds as a deeper commitment to living well. I demand to know myself all the time. This exercise brought me right back to that—completely accepting myself as I am, not how I'm supposed to be or anyone else's ideas of how I ought to be."

The issue of trust drew the following comments from Nancy: "Sometimes I am utterly without trust in the universe. I am empty. Other times, I am absolutely in touch with being in God and of God.

"When I'm in one, I can't believe the other one exists, and I think, 'Oh, that other one's never going to come back.' When I'm in the presence of God I think, 'You've finally got it. You're never going to be in doubt again.' But then I get empty again, and when I'm empty, I'm empty—like a washed-out rag. Sometimes these two feelings come within moments of each other.

"I'm learning to be fully in each of them when they are there. I can't force myself to be God-like when I'm a washrag. That's the challenge for me, to just say, 'This is the way I am right now' and accept that."

* * *

Greg discovered the following attitudes about change: "In the past year I've been very much embracing and flowing with changes that life has been presenting to me. This is the result of a transformation I experienced a year ago when my thirteen-year-old nephew died. It was difficult to accept that no matter how good we were, no matter how loving we were, he was still going to die. But although for him there was no future, he did have his thirteen years and he lived life fully in his way.

"I learned from him. I realized that if I don't live my life today, fully, day by day, I'm not living it at all. I will die with it undone. This has made me willing to take risks, to just be out there experiencing what comes."

Now it's time to add the nutrients necessary to nourish your own soil. *Nourishing your inner soil involves creating affirmations and visualizations that address the growing edges of those core beliefs in need of change.*

Pinpointing your growing edges is the next step in your growth process. The growing edge can have any emotional texture, from scary and confusing to joyful and comforting. When you're on your edge there's always a lot of energy—the energy of new growth coming into existence, much like a bud opening for the first time. It is a state of aliveness and possibility. Implicit in the growing edge is the understanding that one person's edges are not better or worse than another's. They are just different. This understanding frees us of negative self-judgment and allows us to be softer with ourselves.

How do you go about finding your core belief growing edges? You've already discovered a lot through the Inner Soil Test. The next step is to simplify that information and build it into an affirmation and visualization.

To assist you in this process, first look over the following skeleton affirmations to help you identify your own. A skeleton affirmation, with some personalizing, may serve as a foundation for your own unique, self-created affirmation. Put a check next to the ones that speak to you.

- **SELF-RESPONSIBILITY**

Skeleton Affirmations

- I take responsibility to create my life.
- I have the power to change my life.
- I make the choice to grow.
- I have created my past and I will create my future.
- I am the creator of my life.
- The infinite power of the (universe, God, the Creator, etc.) flows through me, helping me create my life.
- I use the full capacity of my mind to manifest my life as I want it.
- I learn from every experience I have in my life.
- My past does not control my future, I do.

- **SELF-ESTEEM**

  Skeleton Affirmations

  - I'm a lovable person.
  - I love myself.
  - I reflect the inner beauty of God.
  - I accept myself fully.
  - I approve of myself fully.
  - I'm capable of doing anything I want.
  - I allow myself to experience the infinite intelligence of the universe.
  - I'm the most wonderful person I know.
  - I tell others how special I am with ease and grace.
  - I always know what to do.
  - I'm worthy of all the abundance the universe has to offer.
  - I'm worthy of love.

- **TRUSTING THE UNIVERSE**

  Skeleton Affirmations

  - I trust the universe as a benevolent place that supports me.
  - I believe in people.
  - I open myself to the universe.
  - I step out into my life with trust.
  - I breathe freely as a child of the universe.
  - I am loved and supported by my creator.
  - God is my friend/father/mother and cares for me.
  - I love playing in my home, the universe.
  - I create my universe every day.
  - I have fun in the universe.

- **POSITIVE ATTITUDE**

  Skeleton Affirmations

  - My life is what I make it.
  - Life flows easily and joyfully for me.
  - My needs are easily met in this world of abundance.
  - I move through life with grace and ease.
  - I enjoy myself in life.
  - My life is abundant with opportunities to contribute meaningfully to the world.
  - I take responsibility to make the world a better place.
  - I succeed in whatever I put my mind to.
  - It can be done.
  - I'll find a way.
  - I love my life.
  - Everyone I meet teaches me.

- Every day my life gets better and better.
- My life is an extraordinary blessing.
- I expect nothing but the best for my life.
- I am grateful for being alive on this beautiful earth.

- **FLOWING WITH CHANGE**

  Skeleton Affirmations

  - I trust that change brings good things.
  - I soften around change, and I am open to its teaching.
  - I am a student of change.
  - Everything is changeable, including my habits.
  - I go gently and patiently with the process of change.
  - I accept that change is a process that doesn't happen all at once.
  - I trust that changes are for my self-betterment.
  - I play with change with a light spirit.
  - I am fluid as a graceful river as I flow with the changes in my life.
  - I embrace change as an essential ingredient in my growth process.
  - I surrender to the flow of change.

You may choose to work with all of your core beliefs, or you may find that only one or two need attention.

As you dig into your core beliefs you may be tempted to create an affirmation and visualization for a pressing issue in a specific life area such as relationships or work. To provide a solid foundation for the work you will do later in this book, it's important that you focus for now only on the core belief level. In later chapters you will have ample opportunity to work with each of the seven vital life areas. The four steps to follow are:

- Review your self-discoveries.
- Identify your growing edge.
- Create your vision.
- Craft your affirmation and visualization.

Refining Your Affirmation and Visualization

Before you start creating your affirmation and visualization, let us share with you several condensed examples from the Empowerment Workshop of people getting on to their growing edge. In the workshop we ask individuals to come in front of the group, share some background on their growing edge, and then state their affirmation and visualization. We then help them refine or deepen it.

LARRY: I chose flowing with change. Instead of being open when a new person or situation comes into my life, I close down and shut myself off. This happens a lot in my work and at home as well. My visualization is me panning for gold and getting very excited as I look in the pan even though I don't know for sure what I will get. This gives me a feeling of being open and accepting of the unexpected. My affirmation is "The unexpected are gold nuggets of opportunity."

US: This is a wonderful image. How can you put you, Larry, in the affirmation and make the idea of "unexpected" more specific?

LARRY: I'd probably do it by seeing myself prospecting, seeking out, and finding gold nuggets. These are opportunities for me instead of feeling that I have to duck everybody that's coming at me. I'm welcoming these golden nuggets into my life. This would be like my visualization of going and panning for gold.

US: Great! So state it with "I."

LARRY: Every day I pan for and welcome golden nuggets of opportunity into my life.

US: How do you feel when you say that?

LARRY: I feel very positive. I feel very good—that it's possible.

US: Do you sense what a creative step you have made? You are now the adventurer in life rather than one who tries to push away changes.

LARRY: Yeah, I feel that I can change the way I act.

US: Thanks, Larry!

KAREN: What I want to work on is self-esteem. I have this big judge that says I'm never good enough. That in order to grow, I have to be self-critical. As I began developing my affirmation I saw myself opening a lid on a bubbling spring. It was a wellspring of goodness and love. In its bigness and depth it could accept all my mistakes and failures. I felt really good about this, but I also felt it wasn't big enough considering how many mistakes and failures it had to accept. Out of this my affirmation became "There is so much bigness in me, I am the biggest of oceans and I accept all of me." My visualization was me sitting by the ocean with my eyes closed and listening to the sound of the waves. I felt the sound and rhythm going through me, with the washing waves and softness healing my heart.

US: Very colorful and vivid. You could get an audio tape of ocean sounds and play it as you are stating this affirmation and seeing your visualization. Do you need the words "there is so much bigness in me"? It seems like the phrase right after that says the same thing. The former phrase is what we call a "buffer," a little safety zone before we leap in. Why don't you try your affirmation without that phrase and see how it feels to you?

KAREN: I realized it was a little long. "I am as big as the ocean and accept all of me as I am." It is much more powerful to me.

US: Take some deep breaths and feel that you are as big as the ocean. Take that into you. Breathe it in. How do you feel?

KAREN: I feel like I am the ocean. I feel vast, capable of holding all of me.

US: Now, Karen, what would be a gesture of acceptance? Create a physical gesture of self-acceptance and self-love.

KAREN: I think I feel myself rocking back and forth. Moving as the ocean sways me.

US: You've chosen one of the most powerful symbols of healing. It would be wonderful to visit the ocean and say your affirmation in front of it. And do your rocking gesture while hearing the sound of the waves. It would help you imprint the new belief you are creating even deeper into your psyche. Thanks!

RITA: My core belief issue is positive attitude. Too many times I look at things as problems. So I've decided that in all weather I'm the sun and it doesn't matter because I can shine on everything.

US: Very powerful image. Again, as in the last example, nature oftentimes gives us the most powerful images for growth and change. When you state the affirmation is there latitude for the days that there are a lot of clouds? We don't want the affirmation to be a setup for a very harsh judgment when you go through the normal ups and downs of being a human being. What causes you not to have a positive attitude?

RITA: Hmm, I don't know. I think the main thing is that I don't feel that I look as I should look. As a result of that, about ten years ago I had some cosmetic surgery. But there are scars and different things that leave me feeling weird. I can hide them and maybe that makes it easier for me to pretend, but I know every day. It's something that I have to try and fight against. And I did learn that the physical isn't as important as deeper things.

US: It's very true and profound. How do you feel now about this?

RITA: I still feel I'm inadequate and don't feel that I look the way I should. I wonder what people will think when they know what I did. I ask myself why I did this thing to myself.

US: You are working with many things here, which means you may need more than one affirmation.

RITA: The whole chart.

US: Yes, the whole chart. We're all working the whole chart, and it's a credit to your commitment to growing that you're willing to face all these issues. Let us for the moment choose one. During the day, what is the issue that comes into your mind most often and causes you to feel negative? There may be a link between several, but choose one.

RITA: I would have to say it's forgiving myself for what I have done to myself.

US: Then this is a major classroom in your life. This is the place that you beat yourself up. If you can shift from concentrating on the negative to the positive here, there's a good chance you can do it in other parts of your life. What would be the words that would say that to you?

RITA: I accept my mistake in this special experience I've created that many don't have a chance to learn?

US: Rather than ''mistake,'' why don't you try ''learning'' and keep it succinct and focused on you instead of others?

RITA: I accept the special learning I've created for myself.

US: This is an act of forgiveness and beyond. It is saying that you take responsibility for the way you've created your life and this is a special way that you've learned and are learning. So will this affirmation assist you during the day when you hear that negative voice in your mind?

RITA: It's a good first step. Now that I've accepted my learning, I need to deal with feeling inadequate.

US: And that's yet another level. For now let us affirm what you've come up with, seeing it as the next step in your healing process. You are looking at a deep issue and you will be able to come at it from different perspectives throughout this journey. So read your affirmation again as you have it and give us your visualization.

RITA: I accept the special learning I've created for myself. And my visualization is me as the sun shining on myself. As I shine on myself I feel positive about myself. I have an inner glow and feel confident and whole.

US: Rita, you've done very courageous work to go so deep. And we know there's more work to do. Thank you very much!

These examples should have given you an opportunity to see some of the subtlety involved in getting your affirmation and visualization on to your growing edge. It's now time for you to create your own unique affirmation and visualization. We wish you much success in your growth.

EXERCISE

Creating Your Affirmation and Visualization

1. Review Your Self-Discoveries:

• Go back over the Inner Soil Test. Write down the core beliefs you want to work on. (If you choose more than one core belief, do steps 2-4 for each one.)

2. Identify Your Growing Edge:

• Go back to the common growing-edge issues you checked off.
• If several of the common growing-edge issues reveal similar characteristics about your worldview, choose the one that most represents you.
• If none of them represented your belief adequately, then state your belief in a short sentence. Knowing what you presently believe will assist you in changing it. Self-awareness is the first step.

3. Create Your Vision:

• Now that you have a clear picture of the present belief that you wish to change, ask yourself: "What do I want? What's a vision that I think might be possible for me?"
• Experiment with free association of words, images, movements, feelings, or anything else that puts you more in touch with your vision. Do

any of the skeleton affirmations you checked adequately describe your vision?

4. Craft Your Affirmation and Visualization:

• Building on your vision or a skeleton affirmation that describes your vision, create your affirmation and visualization.

Following is a review of the guidelines for crafting affirmations and visualizations. Make sure that yours has all these characteristics.

Affirmation:

• Write it down.
• State it in the positive.
• Be succinct.
• Be specific.
• Make it magnetic.
• State it as if it already exists.
• Include yourself in it.
• Have it be about changes in yourself, not others.
• Keep it on the growing edge.

Visualization:

• Evoke feeling.
• Use a single image.
• Include you in the image.
• Make it literal or metaphoric.
• Physically depict it.

Part Two

The
Journey

5

Emotions

$\boxed{C}$ongratulations! You've done all the work necessary to prepare for your journey. You have collected techniques and tools you'll need for a successful trip. Now comes time to start applying them. You are about to go on an adventure to the most interesting, mysterious, surprising destination in the universe—yourself!

Your travel itinerary has seven legs, with each leg taking you on a growth journey through a vital aspect of your life. In this first leg you travel through the feeling part of your life. You explore and uncover that which gives color, texture, and shadowing to your experience of being human. The more in touch you are with your emotions, the more in touch you are with your life. Since emotions pulsate through all the vital areas of life, it's an appropriate place to begin.

For some of us emotions are allies and friends and we use them to connect more deeply with the pulsebeat of our lives. Fear tells us something is wrong. Joy reminds us to be grateful for the miracle of life. Sorrow, love, empathy, compassion, resentment, guilt, reverence, and so on, each tells us something about what's going on inside. We listen to what we're feeling and respond accordingly. We are skillful in working with our emotions.

For others emotions are part of life in which we don't display much understanding or skill. We are uncomfortable with feelings. There are different reasons for this discomfort. Perhaps we live primarily in our intellect and don't know how to connect with what we're feeling. Perhaps our emotions are all locked up inside and we can't express what we're feeling. Perhaps, when we communicate what we're feeling, it comes out in destructive ways. Obviously, none of these ways of dealing with emotions is life-enhancing. On the contrary, these are ways of making ourselves ill. Emotion is energy in motion: e + motion. If we have difficulty in this area of life, we have not learned how to work skillfully with our energy in motion.

To work skillfully with emotions requires that you be able to do three things:

- Feel what you're feeling, and express it in a healthy way—*emotional expression*.
- Change the beliefs causing emotional upsets—*belief work*.
- Let go of negative emotions you have been carrying from the past—*emotional clearing*.

Optimum emotional well-being and health require a partnership of these three ways of working with our emotions.

Let's first look at expressing what you're feeling.

Emotional Expression

We need to be open to our feelings. We need to validate them for what they are—energy within us that is moving. We need to respect them as natural responses to the process of living. They are our humanity speaking to us. We must learn how to listen. When we're feeling sad we need to allow ourselves to cry; when we're feeling angry we need to allow ourselves to yell; when we're feeling joy we need to allow ourselves to exude our jubilance. We also need to find creative ways of expressing these feelings that are not harmful to anyone else.

When a feeling comes up it's very much like water boiling inside a kettle. It requires expression. If it has an opening, it will blow off the steam harmlessly; if it doesn't have an outlet, it will blow its top or burst at the seams. It's up to us to find healthy outlets for the energy in motion that builds up inside us, so we neither have to blow our tops nor wear away our insides.

There are myriad healthy ways to express what you're feeling. Which way you choose depends on the emotion and your personal style. Each of us needs to experiment to discover what works best. We'll share with you some of the ways people we've worked with learned to express their different emotions.

Judith has a special pillow, fondly designated the "anger pillow." When she is upset she lays into that pillow with a vengeance! She punches it, yells at it, and curses it. When she's done there's no anger left—it's all been vented harmlessly into her pillow. This allows her, at a later time, to communicate with the person she's angry with in a calm way. Her only expense is a few pillows each year.

Bill uses a large conga drum to release any kind of emotional upset. He beats his drum until he's physically and emotionally spent.

When Jack is really frustrated by work or family life, he goes on a long run, and this always seems to give him fresh perspective. Nancy uses dance the same way that Jack uses running. When she feels really anxious about something she puts on her favorite dance music and boogies out.

Sometimes Edward feels as if he could burst with joy. For him there's only one way to express this feeling—improvising at the piano. He goes at it until all his joy is expressed. When June is feeling great she loves to sing. She composes her own songs and belts them out.

Vivian knows when she's feeling sad or depressed she needs to sit with a trusted friend or therapist to help her talk it out. She finds the sounding board of another person essential for her emotional health. Arthur uses a different kind of sounding board. He writes what he is feeling in his journal.

These are only some of the many diverse and creative ways we can express and release our emotions. Some methods are physical, some are artistic, others are verbal. No one method of expression is better than another. What's important is that you find a mode or several modes of expression that suit your emotional temperament. Experiment until you find what works best for you.

One cautionary note: As you become more skillful in expressing your emotions, be careful that you don't slip into indulging them. There is a fine line between a healthy, cathartic emotional expression that is healing and a release that happens too often, goes on too long, or is expressed uncontrollably. *Express what you're feeling, then let the feeling go.*

Changing Beliefs That Cause Emotional Upset

As valuable as emotional expression is, it does not bring about any fundamental change in what causes us to get upset. To do this we must go to the root of the upset—what we believe. This is the second part of the three-way partnership of emotional well-being. It is our beliefs that are the cause of all the emotions we feel. If we want to change the pattern that causes us to get emotionally upset, we must change the underlying beliefs.

We feel guilty because we believe we did something wrong. We feel afraid because we believe something bad will happen. How many times have you felt upset about something, afterward found out that you didn't have all the facts, and realized how silly it was to get so upset? What you believed about the situation caused you to become upset. When you believed something new about the situation, the upset vanished. In both cases it was the belief that was at the root of the emotion. *To understand your emotional responses you must understand your beliefs. To change your emotional responses you must change your beliefs.*

Frances, who took our Empowerment Workshop, wrote to us several months later with this story:

"Recently I experienced a long, difficult depression. It was unlike any other I've known. First, it was a surprise—I'd been pretty continuously happy for four months running, then I became quite ill—fever, kidney trouble, bedridden, etc., and when I came out of it, I found myself disoriented. In a little time I found myself in the midst of deep depression.

"So I tried 'staying with it,' tracing it to the root belief causing me to be depressed. In this exploration I recognized a lot of colorful, multifaceted gems in my depression/grief/anger.

"The key one concerned my belief that my work wasn't valid or could even be called work unless it was hard. You know—'work' has to be tedious and painful.... Once I realized what was bothering me, I let go of that silly belief and accepted that it was my right to enjoy my work.

"For the first time in my life I have become happy at my work *and* I still can't think of it as work! The depression has lifted, leaving me in awe of it and myself. I am sturdier and wiser for the experience."

Frances held a deep belief that her work should not be fun, and since it was, she afflicted herself with depression to compensate. Only by unraveling her beliefs was Frances able to heal her depression.

The process of identifying and changing beliefs that are causing you emotional turmoil far out of proportion to outside circumstance is deep inner work and requires a real commitment. Because any belief that causes a painful and inappropriate emotional response has been reinforced so many times, your mind is like a record with a deep groove in it. When the button of your internal record player gets pushed, before you know it that same old tune starts playing, and once again you go through your emotional upset. You seem to have no control over your emotional state; you feel powerless.

This pattern is not inevitable. You can replace the old record with a new one. You can replace the old *unconscious* response with a new *conscious* response.

Changing Beliefs, Changing Responses

The process of creating a new emotional response to a situation has five steps:

1. *Identify* the undesired emotional responses that have persisted for some time. Be aware of the anger, sadness, sharpness, irritation that always seems to come up when your mother/father/spouse/child/boss/employee says or does a certain thing—when they push your "hot button." Your hot button is that sensitive spot in your psyche that has been pushed so often that it is on a hair trigger. You react immediately, unthinkingly, and strongly every time someone touches you there.

For example, you could have a sensitivity to a particular tone of voice your spouse adopts. When you hear that tone of voice you erupt. You might, for instance, hate receiving phone calls while at work from your brother because you know he will waste your valuable time and distract you, yet you cannot plausibly refuse to accept his calls.

2. *Use* the power of that emotional upset to help you track down the words to the old record that goes on when your button is pushed, e.g.:

- I'm not good enough.
- I'm not capable.
- I'm not lovable.
- I'm too busy.
- I don't have the time.
- It's too much trouble.
- I don't know how to say no.
- He/she won't like me.

As you engage in this self-examination each time your button is pushed, you actually use your button as a tool to assist you in delving for your underlying beliefs. This is an excellent way to bring to the surface the unconscious beliefs underlying the emotional response. In this way the emotional response becomes a useful servant of yours rather than your master.

In the case of your brother, you might find that you have an underlying belief that you cannot say "no" to a family member, no matter how outrageous their demands. Going deeper, you might find that you always feel a need to prove yourself to others, that you don't accept your self-worth unless your actions meet with their approval. The energy generated in your interactions with your brother can be used to prompt you to look deeper within to discover the real causes of your reactions. Your underlying belief could thus be stated: "I don't believe in myself without others' approval."

3. Once you have identified the old record that needs to be changed, *create a new record* in the form of an affirmation and visualization to play when your button gets pushed. The new record should be a belief that reverses the former belief, e.g.:

- I am lovable.
- I am capable.
- I am good enough.
- I love my mother/father/spouse/child.
- I have time.
- I am tolerant.
- I am patient.
- I am gentle.
- I am strong.
- I am clear.

Use your own words. Create a visualization of you responding in the exact way you would like. If you would like to be calmer, see yourself calm. If you would like to be angrier, see yourself angry. If you would like to be more tolerant, see yourself patient. If you would like to be more forthright in stating what's on your mind, see yourself clearly saying what you need to say. If you would like to have a sense of humor in the heat of the moment, see yourself telling a joke.

In the case of your brother, you might say "I lovingly and clearly tell my brother what I feel."

4. Now *create a pause function* for your record player. This is a way of giving yourself time to change records when your button gets pushed. Some good pause devices are three deep breaths, visualizing a red stop sign, or literally walking away from the situation for a few moments.

If you do this every time you receive a call from your brother at work, you have the opportunity to repeat your affirmation and gain perspective on the situation before you plunge in. In this case *you* are in control of your responses, not your hot button.

One couple used the words "chopped liver" whenever either of them had their button pushed by the other. This lightened up the situation fast and gave both of them time to pause and put on their new records.

5. *Mentally rehearse your new techniques every day.* See yourself in the situation. Picture your button getting pushed. See yourself at that critical moment of choice—*pausing.* Imagine yourself putting on your new record.

This rehearsal will allow you to be ready when your difficult emotional situation arises. After a while the new record will be the most popular one in your collection and you won't need to do any more rehearsing.

This technique requires a serious commitment to staying conscious and aware in a variety of tough interactions. It requires an attentive look at the habitual emotional responses in your life. Once you have become aware of the change you want to create, you need to be vigilant when you're in the thick of things. We each choose in every moment how we're going to respond. With this technique you'll be able to respond in a life-enhancing way.

EXERCISE

Hot Buttons

Take some time and think about any people or situations that push your button and cause you to get upset. Would you like to respond in a different manner? How you respond is your choice. It isn't easy to change your unconscious emotional response patterns, but it's worth the effort considering the alternative—being run by them for the rest of your life. Use this five-step process to create more emotional calm in your life. Some space has been left for you do to this exercise in case your journal is not handy. (By the way, examine one hot button at a time—most of us have several!)

1. What is my "hot button" (a recurring situation that causes me emotional distress)?

2. What old record goes on when the button is pressed? What is my habitual response?

3. What is the underlying belief behind that response?

4. How would I really like to react? What new record can I create that is filled with positive, life-affirming energy? State this in the form of an affirmation.

5. What is a pause device that will prevent me from becoming emotionally hooked? In your mind, play the record of the situation that pushes your button. When you get to the point where your button gets pushed, put on your pause device. Visualize this.

6. Now visualize putting on your new record and playing that one instead. Rehearse the whole sequence of events in your mind: the situation, the button, the pause, the new record. Rehearse it until the new record is the only record—at which point you'll find you won't need a record at all.

Emotional Clearing

The final part of creating a healthy emotional life is to *let go of the deep hurts that you have been holding on to from the past.* In order to be free and have peace of mind, we have to learn to release the anger, resentment, or bitterness we may feel toward someone who has deeply hurt us or the guilt we may feel about a past mistake.

Perhaps you gave your love to someone and they left you—your heart is broken. Perhaps someone you placed a lot of trust in took advantage of you—you feel betrayed. Maybe your parents mistreated you as you were growing up—you resent them for it your whole life. Perhaps you did something that proved to be a major life mistake or that hurt someone very deeply—so every day you think about this and feel guilty.

Emotional pain is part of the Earth curriculum. It's not good, it's not bad, it's just the way things are. We can't avoid it, but we don't have to spend our lives staying wounded.

Yet it's not always easy to let go of past hurts. They have become quite familiar to us. And for some of us a large part of our identity has been created out of our woundings. In the name of self-righteous indignation we have spent a lot of our precious life energy feeling angry or resentful or bitter toward someone from our past.

Unfortunately, we are the losers. We have emotionally handcuffed ourselves to that person, dragging them with us wherever we go. They are free of us, but we are bound to them. Just think of the freedom you would have if you let go and released that person from your life. And if the person that needs to be released for something done in the past is you, all the more incentive to step forward into emotional freedom.

Why hold on? As one Empowerment Workshop participant said, "I wanted so badly to let go. But although intellectually I wanted it to happen, it just wasn't happening. I woke up this morning and, as I was madly writing in my journal, it finally hit me why I was hanging on to that baggage. It's all wrapped up in my sense that I have no future. I live very much day-to-day and there is a lot of question about my future. I want to hang on to the past because that's the only thing I have.

"Then the whole idea of mental clearing came to me, of finally being able to let it all go, and create a new future free of my emotional baggage."

How do we let go? Here are some guidelines that can assist you in the letting-go process.

Guidelines for Letting Go:

• Letting go of your resentment, anger, or bitterness does not mean that you condone what happened. It simply means that you're releasing the emotional hurt from your life and that you value peace of mind more than being right.

• *Only you* can make the choice to let go of old emotional baggage. Letting go is a choice you make, just as staying hurt is a choice you make. It's up to you.

• Our minds like to hold on to the past. It's comfortable, safe, and known. To let go of the past and step into a new way of being requires inner strength and courage. By letting go you're saying "I'm done with this experience in my life, I'm ready and willing to move on. I now choose to be free."

• The hurts you've suffered in the past *can be released forever at any moment*. They are stuck energy. If you wholeheartedly want to release it, you can. The purpose of life is not meant to continually be a healing of past wounds. As soon as we let go of the past we can use our unstuck energy to create our future.

• If you're unwilling to release a past hurt completely, release as much as you can. We worked with one man who had just completed a painful divorce and didn't feel ready to let go of the anger he felt toward his wife. But he also knew he didn't want to be burdened with constant emotional pain. He felt stuck.

He was a real estate entrepreneur and liked to make deals. We suggested that he cut a deal with himself and decide how much of the anger he wanted to hold on to and how much he would be willing to release. He cut a deal: He held on to 95 percent of his anger and released 5 percent. Subsequently we received two letters from him. The first said, "I've renegotiated—60 percent for me, 40 percent I let go." The next letter said, "I've cut the best deal of my life—I'm letting go of all of it."

• If you've let go of a hurt and you start thinking about it again, just notice it and gently let it go again. Your mind has become used to holding on to this hurt and may periodically recreate it out of habit.

• The most common places we hold on to hurts and resentments are from our parents, past relationships, work, and childhood.

It's time to let go of some old baggage. Before you begin this exercise take a few minutes to reflect on these questions:

• Are you angry, resentful, or bitter toward your parents for anything?
• Do you hold childhood memories of being hurt by anybody that you still carry with you?
• Are there any past lovers or friends who hurt you and toward whom you still feel resentful?
• Do you feel angry or bitter toward a former boss, business associate, or authority figure in your life?
• Do you still harbor feelings of guilt for something you did in the past?

EXERCISE

Guided Visualization: Letting Go

Your work in this exercise is to identify the deep hurts from the past that you are still holding on to and release them so you can be free. Allow thirty minutes to do this exercise. You will not need your journal. Find a quiet place where you will be undisturbed, sit in a comfortable chair, and put on some quiet music. The guided visualization is divided into different parts. When you have completed one part go on to the next. Get ready, and let's begin.

1. Imagine a long tunnel that represents your life. Experience this as a safe and healing tunnel. Experience yourself as courageous and truly ready to let go and be free. Notice that the tunnel starts from the present time and goes all the way back to when you were born. Close your eyes and view the tunnel of your life.

2. In your imagination take a step back into this tunnel, a step that represents the last five years of your life. In this recent past are there any people, including yourself, toward whom you hold resentment, anger, bitterness, or guilt? Close your eyes and identify the people, deceased or alive, if there are any.

3. If there is more than one person, start with one and picture him or her in the healing tunnel with you. Gently begin to relate and communicate your thoughts and feelings to the person. Tell him or her why you felt hurt. Share as fully and honestly as you can. Close your eyes and begin your communication. Let it last as long as necessary to achieve a thorough understanding.

4. Now listen as this person communicates back to you. Allow yourself to fully listen and hear their truth. Take a deep breath and for a few moments consider both truths, his or hers and yours. Close your eyes and listen carefully to the other person.

5. Gently begin to let go of the burden of your resentment toward this person or yourself. Feel your inner strength and courage. Take a deep breath and, in whatever way feels good to you, release this stuck emotional energy. As you release any bitterness or anger you are holding, notice how freeing it is and how light it makes you feel. Close your eyes and experience the release.

6. Repeat steps 3 through 5 for each person from the last five years of your life toward whom you harbor unresolved negative feelings.

7. Go back through your life tunnel at five-year intervals and repeat steps 2 through 6.

8. If you did this exercise wholeheartedly, you are likely to feel lighter and emotionally open. Spend some time with this feeling before you move on. Allow yourself the gift of savoring a tender moment with yourself. To complete this experience imagine your body bathed in healing white light.

6

Relationships

$\boxed{\text{T}}$he next leg of your journey explores the territory of the heart—relating to another whom you love. This is the stuff with which poets have filled volumes. It's exciting and wondrous—it's also scary.

A loving relationship is scary because offering and receiving love from another makes us vulnerable. When we allow another person into our heart we can be rejected and it will be painful. We can be criticized and it will sting. We can hurt another and it will fill us with sorrow. And the depth of inner feeling can be unfathomable with someone we love. A loving relationship takes us to the very depths of being human and demands that we grow.

What does a loving and growing couple relationship look like and how do we create it? To answer this question we'll draw from the many things we've learned in creating our own marriage and work partnership. We'll also draw from what we've learned by witnessing the many remarkable couples who have attended the Empowerment Workshop. Although our primary emphasis is on a committed couple relationship, what is said can, with a little adaptation, be translated to other long-term relationships.

Those of you *seeking* a relationship can use this chapter to clear the patterns that may have obstructed you in the past and to bring out those things in yourself that will assist you in creating a successful long-term relationship.

Guidelines for Creating a Loving, Growth-filled Relationship

• **The First Love Relationship Must Be with Self** Begin by nurturing your primary relationship with self. You must take the time to nurture yourself, to grow and develop as an individual. You must put yourself at the top of the list of important people for whose well-being you are responsible. This doesn't mean narcissism but rather healthy love and nurturing of self.

The more whole you are, the more you can bring to a relationship. When you attempt to have the relationship fill in the gaps and incomplete places inside, you are bound to become frustrated. It puts too much strain on the relationship. Taking the time to nurture yourself is an essential ingredient in the nurturing of your couplehood.

• **Create a Higher Purpose for Your Relationship** When you create a higher purpose for your relationship it gives you a larger context beyond the daily joys and struggles. When things are tough or confusing it helps to remember the vision to which the relationship is dedicated. Some possible higher purposes to which your relationship could be committed might be: a growth or spiritual path to help each other evolve; a way to perform service in the world; to raise a conscious, loving family; to learn how to love. Make up your own words to describe your higher purpose and put them into the form of an affirmation.

- **Commit to Heart-Centered Communication** This is a threefold process:

  - *Speak honestly* of your concerns, fears, and hurts to your partner.
  - *Quiet your internal chatter* so you can listen and deeply hear what your partner is saying to you.
  - *Let go gracefully* of hurts and resentment.

None of this is easy, yet all of it is essential to keeping the communication channels in the relationship clear. With clear channels the love flows smoothly, offering its vitality to both people. Create the time to speak what's in your heart.

- **Integrate the Male and Female Aspects Within You** To create a relationship that is balanced you both need to put forward energy—your male side—and to receive energy—your female side. You both need to be able to put out your ideas, visions, dreams, problems, concerns, and fears, and also to listen, take in, support, nurture, and nourish one another. Both parts make up the whole of who you are and are essential for a mature relationship.

- **Confront Your Power Issues** Inherent in any committed relationship are times when you push against each other. You argue about whose point of view will prevail. Power confrontations are a natural and dynamic part of growth relationships, especially as the roles of women and men continue to change. This is one of the most challenging aspects of the relationship. It demands that both people be willing to express, clearly and firmly, what they want and to confront the struggle head-on.

If either person hides their wants out of fear of confrontation, the relationship can't grow and one person begins dominating the other. We encourage you not to resist or be ashamed of your power struggles. Let them surface. Once the issues are acknowledged, you can work on finding solutions in which you both win. Though it's difficult to accept sometimes, our differences are part of our attraction to each other. They are a major part of how we grow and learn in a relationship.

- **Create Space for Each Individual Within the Relationship** You each need to find time to be alone and separate. Set aside time to nourish your individuality without having to consider the needs of your partner.

This time alone is essential to the health and well-being of the relationship. It's a time to connect with your own spirit. Otherwise each one sacrifices his or her individuality to the couple relationship and both eventually will begin to resent this.

- **Have Fun** If your primary focus is "working" on the relationship, it quickly becomes tedious. Every couple needs healthy doses of joyful play, both play for its own sake and play for the sake of the relationship. The spark that attracted you to each other needs to be regularly rekindled. The romance continually needs the space and time to be recultivated. The best way to do this is to create time to enjoy each other and play together.

• **In Times of Impasse, Get Support** All relationships periodically bog down over some issue. Try as you will to get unstuck, you keep spinning your wheels. This is the time to reach out and ask for help. This can mean asking a trusted couple to offer some perspective. It can mean attending a workshop. It can mean seeking counsel from a therapist.

• **Honor the Continuous Process of Change** Change is inherent in any growing relationship. As each person grows, the dynamics of the relationship must change to accommodate this growth. As each person outgrows old patterns or embarks on new visions, the relationship must adjust. Outside factors like work, family, and culture are also continually impinging on the relationship and triggering change. To keep the relationship alive and vital each partner must overcome the tendency to want to keep things the way they have always been, to maintain the status quo. Successful couples stay attentive to their joint growing edges and honor change as a natural part of the relationship.

• **Renew Your Respect for Each Other** In the early stages of most relationships we are careful to treat our partners respectfully. We listen to them carefully, don't interrupt them while they're talking, and are considerate of their feelings. As the relationship gets older we tend to get sloppy in how we treat the person we love. We sometimes find ourselves saying and doing things that are hurtful. We expect and assume that our partner will stick around and that this gives us license to take advantage of their love and trust.

As a daily practice think of your loved one as you would your best friend. Create an affirmation that reminds you how deeply you value your friend, an affirmation that you always remember when you are together. Create an affirmation that will be true of the quality of your relationship a year or a decade hence.

Whenever you are with your partner remember this affirmation. When you are tempted to let fly with your resentment or anger, think instead of the affirmation and the validation of your partner's nature that it inspires in you. Let this affirmation be an enduring symbol of the respect you have for your partner.

• **Embrace the Paradox** A relationship is the master teacher of paradox. The person we love the most we often hurt the most. In a very brief period of time we can experience intense joy and intense pain. There are times we can't live without this person and times when we can't live with them. There are times when the relationship offers us the most profound sense of stability—and, around the next corner, utter chaos and insecurity.

These kinds of paradoxes pervade the reality of relationship. If we are to be in relationship, we need to accept and embrace them. The stronger the relationship's commitment to growth and love, the easier it can bend when the winds blow.

Vulnerability:
The Heart of a Growth Relationship

As you looked at these guidelines you probably noticed how many times honest communication came up as an essential ingredient of a growth relationship. It is the vital fluid that allows a relationship to be alive.

The essence of honest communication is vulnerability. It is the willingness to share the most fragile and tender parts of yourself with another. It is the willingness to talk about your deepest fears, self-doubts, and yearnings. It takes courage to allow your innermost feelings to be seen by another. It's scary. There's no guarantee your partner won't reject you.

So why take the chance of being rejected? The answer is because it allows you to take the relationship a quantum leap forward. When you risk in this way you open yourself to love, support, and healing from another. You allow yourself to trust another human being. You allow another to enter intimately into your life. This is a profound experience and a blessing for both people. Let us share with you a story about vulnerability.

There was this guy named David, and he had a healthy dose of male enculturation. He was taught that you don't show anybody parts of yourself that you're not sure about. You certainly need to put your best foot forward if you're going to win the heart of a fair maiden. Then he met a fair maiden named Gail and fell madly in love with her. Fortunately, for him, the feeling was mutual.

After several months of seeing each other, Gail told David, "I'm afraid that you may reject me because I'm not good enough." This surprised David, because he thought she was fantastic, everything he had ever hoped for. Gail continued to have her moments of insecurity and shared them freely with David. Every time she did that David felt closer to Gail and respected her more for her sharing. He also said to himself, "My God, I never would share such stuff. If she knew I wasn't totally together, she might reject me. I better keep putting my best foot forward."

Meanwhile, David started having his own fears and insecurities squirming around inside. Finally, after a few more months passed, during which Gail continued to freely share her deepest concerns about not being good enough, David got up the courage to tell Gail that he also had some fears. He told her he was afraid she might reject him for someone else. He told her he had been rejected in a past relationship and was afraid he might get rejected again. He told her that he was head over heels in love with her and it was scary to be so out of control. Each time he shared these deep things he took a breath and hoped that she wouldn't walk away.

To his surprise and complete joy she responded with great caring. She acknowledged that it must have been hard for him to overcome his past conditioning and speak so vulnerably. She told him that she loved him all the more and had no intention of leaving him.

David began realizing that as he opened up his fears of rejection to Gail, her love was helping to heal them. He started feeling that not only was it safe to be vulnerable with Gail, it actually helped heal his fears. His fear that Gail would think less of him if he shared his insecurity was gone. With nothing to hide or protect, he began openly discussing and healing his other deep fears about the relationship. Eventually the relationship moved to a place where they both felt safe at any time sharing what was really in their hearts.

As a result of their acts of vulnerability, Gail and David came away with greater acceptance of themselves and each other. They grew and the relationship flowered.

If you want your most intimate relationship to grow and flourish, you must work to heal and transform the deepest fears you hold about it. The *first step in this process is discovering your fears* and beginning your internal healing and transformation process. The second step is being willing to share these fears with the one you love. This next exercise will be an opportunity to take that first step of discovering and healing your fears.

Healing Relationship Fears

You will soon begin healing and transforming the deepest fears you hold about a loving, committed relationship. These are the fears that make you feel most vulnerable. Fear and vulnerability are not easy things to face, and there are all sorts of ways we can trick ourselves out of coming to terms with these issues. For that reason we're including a list of common fears to help you get through that first mental block; then, as part of the exercise, we'll help you overcome the many resistances that may come up when you come close to expressing your vulnerability.

The first part of the exercise is a guided visualization to help you bring to the surface your fears about relationships. You then will choose the fear that is most core and come to understand it better. Then you'll be guided to transform that fear into a vision of how you would like it to be. You'll create your vision in both image and affirmation.

In the second part of the exercise you will list any resistances you have to believing in your affirmation. This is a powerful mental clearing tool that will allow you to bring to the surface the old, unconscious mental programming, which might otherwise sabotage your affirmation.

One woman had the following experience during this process: "After my marriage dissolved I felt badly betrayed by someone I had really believed in. Since then I've pretty much slammed and bolted the door that leads to new relationships.

"I wanted to turn this fear around. The first affirmation that I came up with was 'I can have intimate, vulnerable relationships because I have discrimination and wisdom.'

"Going deeper into my resistances, I realized that I am not open to being hurt. Yet if I'm to be vulnerable, I have to be open to being hurt. Going deeper still, I realized that being hurt is such a devastating experience because my self-esteem is destroyed. This is why it was so painful when my marriage fell apart. I was not strong, wise, or whole.

"So the final affirmation I came up with is 'I rejoice in my strength and my wisdom and my wholeness and I allow intimate, vulnerable relationships into my life.'

"Because of all the pain that went before, I can now really own these new qualities."

Common Fears

A list of common fears about relationships appears below, along with affirmations some people have found helpful in addressing those fears. These will prime the pump a bit and help you get at your own fears.

FEAR: My partner will leave me when he/she finds out who I really am.
AFFIRMATION: I affirm all of my humanity and know that the deepest way of being loved is by being fully known.

FEAR: I am not deserving of a loving relationship.
AFFIRMATION: I am a unique and totally lovable person and deserve all the gifts of a wonderful, loving relationship.

FEAR: I won't find anyone who meets my requirements as an ideal partner.
AFFIRMATION: If God could come up with someone like me, I'm sure there's another one around who can match me. I attract that person to me.

FEAR: The person I love will leave me.
AFFIRMATION: I feel whole and complete exactly as I am and attract into my life someone committed to a long-term relationship.

FEAR: I'll be hurt if I open my heart in the relationship.
AFFIRMATION: I embrace the paradox of relationship—pain and joy. I learn from both of them.

FEAR: I will lose my independence and individuality and get trapped in the relationship.
AFFIRMATION: I choose a partner who supports my independence and individuality, and together we balance being together and being apart.

FEAR: My relationship will be just like my parents' relationship.
AFFIRMATION: I create my own truth in my relationship. I am free of the past.

FEAR: My partner will be just like my mother/father.
AFFIRMATION: I heal my relationship with my mother/father and attract a partner who is appropriate for me.

FEAR: My relationship won't work out.
AFFIRMATION: I trust that I am clear enough to choose wisely and commit to keeping the relationship alive and growing.

FEAR: I will be controlled in the relationship.
AFFIRMATION: I own my own power and choose a partner who is empowering.

FEAR: My partner will not be faithful.
AFFIRMATION: I choose a partner committed to monogamy.

FEAR: My partner will be attracted to other men/women.
AFFIRMATION: I accept the attraction of my partner to other people as natural and healthy. I encourage and support my partner and myself to develop other friendships.

FEAR: Relationships are too complex in this day and age and are doomed to fall apart.
AFFIRMATION: Relationships work when love and the willingness to grow are present. I create a loving, growing, and totally successful relationship.

EXERCISE

From Fear to Vision

Allow approximately thirty minutes to do this exercise. You will need your journal and some colored pens or other drawing materials. Space has been left in case you don't have your journal handy. Find a quiet place where you will be undisturbed. Sit in a comfortable chair and put on some soft, relaxing music.

The guided visualization is divided into several parts. At certain points you will be guided to close your eyes so you can more easily visualize. After each visualization, draw or record your perceptions in your journal.

Remind yourself to maintain soft eyes as you move back and forth between your imaginative and ordinary states of mind. Get ready for this inner exploration.

1. Take a few deep breaths and feel the courage within you to explore your heart. Close your eyes and visualize your courage. One way of connecting with your heart is to place a hand over your heart area.

2. Go into your heart and begin discovering those fears that you're most afraid of telling someone you love. Make note of the fears that apply to you. The following questions may help you.

    a. It is most difficult for me to tell someone I love that I am afraid of:

        rejection
        abandonment
        betrayal
        loss of freedom
        loss of self
        not being deserving of love

_____

_____

_____

    b. What is it that causes you to contract, to pull away, in your intimate love relationship?

    c. What situations seem to cause these fears to come up? Write down your observations.

3. Keep going deeper into these fears and see if there is one fear that seems to embrace the other fears, one fear that is at the core. See if a particular fear seems to be the worst. Then write down what you're afraid might happen. Record in your journal, with soft eyes, what you discover.

4. Keep going deeper into that fear. What does the fear look like? What color is it? What texture is it? What shape is it? Close your eyes and visualize and experience the fear. Using colored pens or pastels, draw a picture of the fear.

5. How does looking at this fear make you feel? Write down the words that come to you. Then ask the fear, "Why have I created you in my life? What do you have to teach me?" Reflect on these questions. Record your answers in your journal.

6. You created your fear. It is just as possible for you to create the most ideal circumstance for yourself that you can imagine. How would you like things to be? What is your vision of what lies on the other side of the fear? What does this vision look like? What image captures the feeling of this vision? What words describe how this vision allows you to feel? See yourself moving through your fear and fully becoming one with your vision. Draw the image and record the words that describe your vision.

7. Allow this vision, and all the insight you have generated, into your heart. Breathe in and experience this expanded feeling. Do this several times. Then translate your vision into an affirmation of how you would like your relationships to be. Write it down.

8. After you have created your affirmation do the following resistance clearing process. Clear as many layers of resistance as you can.

a. Now that you have written down your affirmation, write down any resistances you have to believing it. For example, if your core fear is rejection, your affirmation might be "I accept myself and share who I am totally." Your resistance to believing this might be "No way, I'll get hurt if I fully open myself to someone." Now, instead of negating the resistance, which only energizes it more by giving it mental attention, reaffirm your affirmation and give *it* your mental energy. Once again, write down your affirmation. You then write down the next resistance that comes up for you. The next resistance that comes up might be "Forget it, no one will love me when they really get to know me."

b. Do this five times. You'll discover it's like peeling the layers of an onion. You peel off one resistance and notice another, more subtle resistance underneath. Because you are working with a deeply ingrained fear, it takes time to peel away the resistances to believing your new affirmation. Don't forget to reaffirm your affirmation each time you write a resistance.

c. If after five times you still find your resistance is very strong, you need to back up, for you are beyond your growing edge. Using the first example, perhaps the affirmation might need to be "I accept myself," leaving out the phrase "and share who I am totally." *Use your resistances as feedback and adjust your affirmation accordingly.*

9. Now write down your final affirmation.

Enjoy your new growth. See you on the next leg of the journey!

7

Sexuality

The deepest impulse we possess is our sexuality. It is a powerful and primal force. It can be used not only to bring new life into existence but to regenerate our present life with passion and creativity. When we do not express our sexuality our life force stagnates and our vital energies dissipate.

The full expression of our sexuality lies not in the mastery of mechanical techniques for inducing pleasure but rather in loving, intimate, sensual, sacred engagement with life. Engagement with life sees love as the gift that makes lovemaking a joyous act. Engagement with life draws out our passion and inspires us to make it happen. Engagement with life acknowledges that the divine energy that animates the universe is the same energy that animates us. Willingness to fully share our life force is the most intimate union we can experience—this is true sexuality.

We often stifle our sexuality by limiting the vision with which we define it. In our culture sexuality is defined as the act of intercourse; for some it gets even more narrow and is seen exclusively as the orgasm. Sam Keen speaks eloquently to this: "Our bodies have become erotic deserts, deprived of the multitude of sensory delights. And the genitals are assigned the role of oasis in a wasteland of pleasure. We expect the flowering of sex to make up to us for a desecrated life of the senses."

Why not expand your love life from the single arena of the bedroom to all of life? Why not allow your sexuality to become your love for life, so that you make love not only to your partner, but also to the mountain you climb, the flowers you arrange, your work, and your spiritual quest? When defined in this fuller way your sexuality is your passion for living the whole of your life.

Let's begin exploring your passion by going to its source—what you believe. What does sexuality look like for you?

Sexual Beliefs

As we have been saying again and again, what you believe is what you get. What do you believe about your sexuality? How much of what you believe reflects who you are today—and how much is outdated past programming?

Most of your attitudes about sexuality are unconsciously received from your parents, friends, religion, *Dallas*, past lovers, Madison Avenue, and society at large. In some cases these beliefs reflect your true sexuality, and you should hold on to them. In other cases you have picked up beliefs that are inhibiting or limiting your sexual expression, beliefs that are not true of who you are today. You need to remove them, to weed your mental garden. Most of us have accumulated a surprising number of unnoticed weeds over the years.

This process of sorting out what is true for you is obviously important, yet not always easy given the complex times we live in. The sexual revolution opened up many doors, eliminated many taboos, and presented us with a variety of sexual life-style options and belief systems from which to choose. People today are deciding whether to be heterosexual, homosexual, bisexual, monogamous, celibate; whether or not to start off a relationship by discussing AIDS; whether to have a child or not have a child. It sure ain't like it used to be.

The process of sorting through what you believe and what you do not believe to determine what represents your own unique truth is an extraordinarily empowering act. It is a declaration to yourself that you are willing to take complete responsibility for creating your life. Inherent in this process is asking yourself "What do I value? What do I want?" What for one person is a limiting belief may for another be the deepest truth.

For example, one person might believe that it is important to be monogamous if you are married but not important if you are just dating or living with someone. Another person might believe that a commitment to live together is the same as marriage and thus fidelity is essential. Still someone else might believe that one should be able to engage in lovemaking outside of these relationships.

Monogamy is just one of any number of sexual issues that can be discussed with persuasive arguments on all sides. We live in a time and a culture that leave us free to find our own truth. The main point is, though, that *the rules we live by must truly be our own*. They must reflect our deepest being. They must be expressions of who we are. If we adopt standards that come to us from someone else's value system, they will not be our own no matter how coherent and well intentioned they are. As we bring each of our beliefs into this kind of scrutiny, we sort out which of them are truly ours and which have been imposed by our own fears or outside agents.

The next exercise will help you identify and overcome these limitations. We'll begin by looking at some examples of what some people have discovered as their limiting beliefs about sexuality.

Examples of Limiting Sexual Beliefs

- The only way to make love is to have orgasm.
- I cannot enjoy sexual pleasure by myself.
- It is more important that my partner get pleasure from sex than for me.
- Long-term relationships are fated to become sexually boring and lack passion.
- Communicating what I want takes away spontaneity in lovemaking.
- My partner will not think I am sexually attractive because my body is not nice enough.
- Having preferences as to which sexual acts I like is a sign of inhibition.
- I have been hurt in past sexual relationships and I will be hurt again if I am intimate.

- My sexual desire rhythm isn't normal.
- As a woman, if I express my sensuality, men will take it as a sexual invitation.
- As a man, I always have to initiate and perform in lovemaking.
- With the AIDS epidemic, sex can't be fun anymore.

Turning Limiting Beliefs Around

Once you have identified your limiting beliefs and attitudes, the next step is to replace them with new, more expanded beliefs. These new attitudes take off your mental blinders and open up your view. We call this mental clearing technique the "turnaround" process. You take your limiting idea and expand it to include a broader perspective. Other ways to think about this process include expanding your context, reframing your ideas, or reinterpreting your reality. A *turnaround often takes you out of either/or narrow thinking and frees up your imagination.* Becoming more open-minded, you see your options in terms of both/and.

Some sexual limiting beliefs may weigh large in your life and emerge as the growing-edge issues you choose to work with in the exercises at the end of this chapter, while others are just weeds to remove and be done with. Following are the turnarounds created by the people whose limiting beliefs we shared above.

Turnaround Examples

LIMITING BELIEF: The only way to make love is to have orgasm.
TURNAROUND: What I want from lovemaking is intimacy, deep caring, and union. Sometimes this includes orgasm.

LIMITING BELIEF: I cannot enjoy sexual pleasure by myself.
TURNAROUND: The simple passion of enjoying sexual pleasure is available to me at any time. I am the master of my own sensual/sexual enjoyment.

LIMITING BELIEF: It is more important that my partner get pleasure from lovemaking than for me.
TURNAROUND: Lovemaking is a dance of mutual pleasure and union for me and my lover. I take responsibility to offer and receive sexual pleasure.

LIMITING BELIEF: Long-term relationships are fated to become sexually boring and lack passion.
TURNAROUND: The level of passion and vitality in my sex life is a direct reflection of my commitment to continually opening deeper parts of myself and to my commitment to being fully passionate and alive in the rest of my life.

LIMITING BELIEF: Communicating what I want takes away my spontaneity in lovemaking.
TURNAROUND: The more I share what I want, the more fun lovemaking is for me.

LIMITING BELIEF: My partner will not think I am sexually attractive because my body is not nice enough.
TURNAROUND: I love all of myself and offer my partner my full radiant being.

LIMITING BELIEF: Having preferences as to which sexual acts I like is a sign of inhibition.
TURNAROUND: I am unique in my sexuality, with the right to decide what I do and do not enjoy.

LIMITING BELIEF: I have been hurt in past relationships and I will be hurt again if I am intimate.
TURNAROUND: I have the wisdom and discrimination to use my past experiences to wisely create intimacy in a new relationship.

LIMITING BELIEF: My sexual desire and rhythm aren't normal.
TURNAROUND: I discover and trust my unique sexual rhythms.

LIMITING BELIEF: As a woman, if I express my sensuality, men will take it as a sexual invitation.
TURNAROUND: I make sure I am clear what message I'm putting out and my energy speaks for itself.

LIMITING BELIEF: As a man, I always have to initiate and perform in lovemaking.
TURNAROUND: I create my own standard of what gives me satisfaction.

LIMITING BELIEF: With the AIDS epidemic, sex can't be fun anymore.
TURNAROUND: I take responsibility to make sex safe and fun.

A few parting words before you go off, mental hoe in hand, to crawl around weeding your garden:

These turnarounds are stepping-stones to creating affirmations. Their primary purpose is to clear the garden of weeds. They can be stated more loosely than an affirmation.

You may not fully believe all of your turnarounds right away. It takes time. And, as you know through all the inner work you have done so far, it is the creating of a new belief that causes the change to start.

As you do this next exercise, pay attention to what was told or not told to you by your mother and father; notice what was communicated by religion, past friends, and lovers; think carefully about the constant barrage of messages from television and films. Notice the things that you believe about the act of lovemaking, about intimacy, sensuality, and your passion for life—how you express your life force.

In the upcoming exercise be aware that some of your limiting beliefs will be more superficial, while others will be deep-rooted and tougher to turn around. You may also discover that you do not have a lot of weeds, that the sexuality part of your mental garden is clear. If this is the case, celebrate your clear garden and prepare to cultivate anew. Do be careful, however, of your garden *seeming* clear only because you have not thoroughly examined it.

EXERCISE

<u>Turnarounds</u>

Allow twenty to thirty minutes to do this exercise. You will need your journal. Space has been left in case you don't have it handy.

1. Write down your limiting beliefs about sexuality. First concentrate just on your limiting beliefs and do not think about their turnarounds.

2. When you feel you have written down all the limiting beliefs that you can find, start turning them around. Start with the ones that are most important to turn around. Don't worry if you can't turn each one around perfectly, just do the best you can.

Sensuality:
The Ever-Present Invitation

One of the primary ways we express our sexuality is through our sensuality. We can experience our sexuality each time we see a bird in flight, hear a brook gurgling, smell the fragrance of a flower, taste the subtle seasoning of exotic food, or dance with the blood pulsating through our bodies. It is in these ways that our sexuality becomes an integral part of our daily life, giving us continual delight and pleasure. It is not a separate act, divorced from daily living, isolated in time, confined to a bedroom and dependent on a partner. As exquisite as the lovemaking act is, there is much more available to us as sexual beings. One of the most joyous ways we experience our aliveness is through our senses.

What an extraordinary gift we could give ourselves if each day we decided to smell one rose! Experiencing a rose is an erotic experience. The flower's physical beauty first captures the eye—the softness of its texture, the grace of its petals, the subtlety of its color. Soon the most delicate of fragrances wafts through your nostrils and you feel compelled to bring your nose right to the rose, taking in a deep breath of its perfume.

Sensual interaction with life is available to us all day long, every day of our lives. We can reawaken our senses by just knowing that they are there. We can take our involvement with life a step further by engaging our senses with creativity and passion. To dance with trees, sing with birds, and cavort with clouds is to have a sexual relationship with life. In these acts we experience the union of our life force with the life force of all creation. We merge our individuality with the individuality of life itself.

EXERCISE

Sensuality

In this exercise your job is to totally indulge your senses. You are to relive at least two of the most sensually exciting experiences you have ever had. You will recreate your most exciting sensual experiences in your mind, enhancing them to be even better. The purpose of this exercise is simply to have fun by engaging your senses as fully as possible.

To inspire your memory and imagination, here are a few snapshots of some favorite scenes:

- The feeling of running on a hot day, then cooling off in a lake.
- Making love on a beach.

- Climbing a mountain on a clear, crisp fall day.
- Working in a vegetable and herb garden that has just come into full bloom.
- Experiencing the full delight of a gourmet meal under the stars.
- The first-time sights, smells, sounds, and tastes of a new culture.
- Skiing on fresh powder snow.
- Holding a newborn baby.

1. Recreate one of your favorite sensual experiences from your past in your mind, paying very close attention to what is happening to each of your senses. See, smell, touch, hear, and taste everything. Become aware of secondary sensations you may not have been paying attention to at the time. If you were seeing, imagine the sounds. If you were smelling, what were the tastes? As you get fully into the scene, feel free to embellish, exaggerate, and fantasize about how you could make it even better. Write the experience down in detail.

2. Now choose a second scene to remember and enhance. Fully engage and delight your senses. Write down your experiences.

See if you can bring sensually pleasing things into your life on a more regular basis. Reprioritize your life so that sensually enjoying yourself is at least as important as doing all your tasks and fulfilling your responsibilities. It's your life—have fun with it!

Lovemaking

With this fuller view of sexuality let's not forget the lovemaking act itself. With a mental attitude that reflects your clarity, a deepened passion for life, and an awakened sensuality, you will inevitably find that lovemaking expands too.

If lovemaking could be any way you wanted it, how would you have it be? Letting your imagination soar, what does *making love* to another look like? It's time to open up your range of possibility to explore the realms of deep intimacy, sensual rapture, merger with another, the sharing of the life force, and the offering and receiving of pleasure.

As we know well, thought creates. Once you create the vision, you set the stage for reality to follow. The clearer your vision, the more easily it can begin to manifest. The next exercise is designed to bring images of your ideal lovemaking scene to the surface of your mind. Let go of any preconceived notions of how it should be. Let your own truth be the guiding voice. Keep your heart open, your senses alive, and your passion flowing.

EXERCISE

Lovemaking

Allow approximately twenty minutes to do this exercise. You will need your journal. Space has been left in case you don't have it nearby. Find a quiet place where you will be undisturbed. Sit in a comfortable chair and put on some soft, relaxing music. There are eight questions to assist you in creating your vision. Record your response after reading each question. To help you stay inward and in touch with your feelings, images, and thoughts, use soft eyes as you record your responses.

Let your sexuality freely express itself—and have a great time!

1. Begin to visualize the ideal setting or environment for your lovemaking. Where are you? What is special about the setting? Are there any things that you want to include in your setting?

2. As you are entering into your ideal lovemaking experience, how do you feel about yourself:
    a. Physically

    b. Emotionally

c. Mentally

d. Spiritually

3. How do you feel about your partner as you create this special act together?
a. Physically

b. Emotionally

c. Mentally

d. Spiritually

4. In your ideal vision, how is lovemaking initiated?

5. What happens in the early stages of your lovemaking experience? What words, communications, gestures, activities, and qualities make this early phase fulfilling for you?

6. As you move into the main phase of your ideal lovemaking session, what happens? What communications, gestures, activities, and qualities make this part of your experience fulfilling?

7. How do you bring closure on your lovemaking experience so that the completion is ideal?

8. Gently review the entire ideal lovemaking experience you just created and ask yourself: What made this experience meaningful for me?

Here are a few comments by people who did this exercise:

"What happened for me before the lovemaking was just as important as what happened during. It's also the thing that in real life I leave out most often. We went for a walk on the beach and collected treasures and played tag and told jokes and tackled each other in the sand. This was the setup, the place for me to 'connect.' "

"I went to a place where nature surrounds me, a familiar place that means a lot to me. I made love there a long time ago. What was important was that I was outside and I could commune with nature. I could feel God and nature coming through me, and in that feeling I could let everything else go."

"We were in a glass room—I like the comfort of a bed and being in a warm place. The full moon was shining down through us and there was this feeling of connection with the universe. We did a dance together first, which brought an element of spiritual union that colored the lens of the lovemaking experience."

Creating an Affirmation and Visualization on Your Sexual Growing Edge

By now you know a fair amount about your sexuality. It's time to synthesize the work you've done and focus your insights into the specific next step for growth—an affirmation and visualization that addresses your growing edge for sexuality.

To spark you, here are a few actual affirmations and visualizations created by people in our Empowerment Workshop and some of the process they went through in creating them.

Barbara learned her biggest limiting belief was her fear of asserting her needs while making love. She had a limiting belief that she would turn a man off if she asked for what she wanted. She learned in the lovemaking exercise that what was particularly important to her in love-making was to feel cared for and to feel good about herself. Building on these insights, she created this affirmation: "I love myself and ask for what I need in lovemaking." Her visualization was communicating her needs lovingly and clearly to her partner.

Bill discovered in the limiting-beliefs exercise that he had a belief that if he was not currently in a sexual relationship, his sexuality was dead. He was also clear that he was not interested in one-night stands. Using turnarounds and the sensuality exercise, he discovered that his sexuality was quite alive—it was being expressed through the passion he had for his work and his daily interaction with nature. After this self-discovery Bill created the following affirmation: "My sexuality is passionately alive and I nourish it daily." His visualization was walking through the woods by his house with his senses fully interacting with everything around him. In this way he released the narrow definition his culture had placed on sexuality.

EXERCISE

It's time to create your own sexuality affirmation and visualization.

1. Go back and review your limiting beliefs and turnarounds, your exploration of sensuality, and your ideal lovemaking scenario.

2. Synthesize what you have learned from these exercises and then ask yourself, "What is the most important next step in my sexual growth? What is my growing edge?"

3. From the insight you have generated, create your affirmation and visualization. My affirmation for sexuality is:

My visualization for sexuality is:

We leave you with this insight from Shirley about the quality of her experience many months after doing these exercises: " 'Significance' has taken on new meanings for me. What used to be so significant in my life—wanting a man to call me, needing to have something to do on Friday night, etc.—is now relatively insignificant. What used to be somewhat insignificant is now extremely significant. Is it really just lately that birds started flying above me as I drive to work? Is it really just lately that the sun has begun to rise and set so beautifully?

"What is certain is that I have really begun to live life, fully and consciously."

In closing this chapter of our journey together, we hope you have drunk deeply of your passion. May your love life and your love of life be as one.

8

Body

Your body is the most miraculous creation you possess. It creates and brings forth new physical life. It allows you to experience the sensual pleasures and delights of the earth. It transports you around on the planet. It gives you the opportunity to express joy through dance, movement, and play. It allows you to have the experience of physical health and vitality. It helps define your personal identity. It allows you to express your ideas, feelings, and visions. It allows you to physically experience the life energy that flows throughout the universe. It allows you to learn the lessons of the earth and, through them, grow and evolve. Our bodies are our sacred homes.

What images come to your mind when you think about your body? Do you have a relationship with it? How do you want your body to look, to feel, to perform? Do you have a vision for it? Is your body well cared for? Do you have a plan for maintaining it in good working condition?

In this part of the journey you will come into a conscious relationship with your body and create a vision of how you would like it to be. You will work from the inside out. With a clear vision that represents your truth for your body—not someone else's truth—you will discover how to manifest that vision by creating a body well-being program personally suited to you.

If you have a healthy, fit, well-cared-for body that you experience as a source of pride, you'll be able to soar to the next level. If you do just enough basic maintenance to get by, treating your body like a utility car, you'll find inspiration to trade up. And if thus far you've only experienced your body as the thing that carries your head around, you'll find encouragement and hope.

A Dialogue with Your Body

There's no time like the present to get to know your body better. You learned how important good communication is in having a successful relationship. Now what about good communication with your body? Have you ever stopped to ask it what it thinks about things you're doing or not doing to it? It has a consciousness of its own and would be happy to tell you how it's feeling. All you need do is ask. When you do ask be ready for a lively response. Your body may speak to you with humor, poignancy, sadness, anger, compassion, joy—you name it. Your relationship with your body is a totally personal one, and it evolves over time. It's like making a new friend.

It's time to check in and see what your body has to say. Drawing out your body's wisdom and learning from it is a very special act. We hope you enjoy it.

EXERCISE

Body Dialogue

Allow approximately twenty minutes to do this exercise. You will need your journal. Space has been left in case your journal is not handy. It is most helpful to do this exercise with the attitude of a compassionate witness, since we often tend to be quite judgmental about our bodies.

The body dialogue has eleven questions. After each question close your eyes so you can get more in touch with your body. Once you receive an answer from your body, write it down. Remember to keep your eyes soft and relaxed as you do the writing. Find a quiet place where you will be undisturbed. Sit in a comfortable chair and put on some soft, relaxing music.

Get yourself ready for a chat and take a few deep breaths to relax. In your own words tell your body that you would like to have a frank heart-to-heart dialogue and that you want honest feedback about how it's feeling. Ask your body the following questions:

1. How much have I tapped into your overall potential, and how do you feel about this?

2. Are you in good condition, and how do you feel about this?

3. Is your heart and cardiovascular system healthy? How do you feel about this?

4. How flexible and aligned (the health of the spine) are you? How do you feel about this?

5. How do you like the food I put into you? Be specific.

6. Do you have good stamina and endurance? How do you feel about this?

7. Do you have good muscle tone and strength? How do you feel about this?

8. Do you get the appropriate amount of rest? How do you feel about this?

9. Do you feel loved, cared for, and appreciated? How do you feel about this?

10. Is there anything else you would like to say to me before this dialogue is over?

11. Finally, communicate to your body anything you'd like to tell it.

Generally, people are amazed by what they learn, for our bodies are storehouses of information—available for the asking. We hope you received some useful information that you can begin to take action on and began a rapport with your body that you can build upon. As you get more tuned in to your body, it will tell you when to slow down, eat differently, change your exercise pattern, get more rest, or give it more love and appreciation. It can be a trusted and loyal friend if you choose to cultivate the friendship. As you draw on your body's wisdom it will tell you what needs to be done to create physical well-being.

A Body Vision

Let's use the body knowledge you have just gained to build a vision. If your body could be any way *you* would like it to be—not society's vision but *your* vision—what would it look like? What would it feel like? How would it perform? What would it be like to live in an optimally healthy and functioning body?

How you want your body to be is your choice. As you know, our thoughts create, and perhaps nowhere is this more tangibly evident than in our bodies. Your present body is a direct reflection of the beliefs you hold about it. It reflects your beliefs—right down to chronic aches and pains and excess pounds. It is our minds that create the physical reality we experience. If you don't have a positive, clear vision of how you want your body to be, it will "embody" your unconscious beliefs.

EXERCISE

Body Visioning

Allow approximately fifteen minutes to do this exercise. You will need your journal at the end of the exercise.

Find a quiet place where you will be undisturbed. Sit in a comfortable chair or lie on the floor and put on some energetic music that inspires you to want to move. Our favorite for this exercise is "Chariots of Fire" by Vangelis.

Allow each phrase or section you are visualizing to really go deep into your body before you go on to the next. Experience this exercise sensually and physically. If your body starts wanting to express the beat of the music by pulsating or swaying, go with it—this is a high-energy experience. Allow your body to tell you what to do.

Find your music and get yourself set!

1. Allow the energy of the music to pulsate through your body. Feel the beat, feel the pulse. Feel your energy starting to move through your body. Feel your body moving with the energy of the music.

2. Experience your body's energy and vitality. Feel each and every cell pulsating and dancing with energy. Experience your body humming and singing with vitality. Feel its boundless energy and vitality. See this vitality sparkling all over your body and radiating out from you.

3. Experience your body's strength. Feel your physical strength. Allow yourself to experience your body as having all the strength you desire to do anything you desire. Experience your body lifting, climbing, paddling, rowing, or whatever you choose, with all the strength you could possibly need available to you. Experience your body's strength. Feel it. How does it feel? Allow this feeling into your body. Let it go deep into your cells.

4. Experience your body's endurance and stamina. Allow yourself to fully take in and experience your body's capacity to dance as long as it desires— all day long and all night long if you so choose; to run or swim or hike or walk or bike or mountain climb or ski as long as you would like. Feel the capacity of your heart and lungs to pump the energy you need throughout your body. Feel your endurance. Experience your body's boundless stamina.

5. Experience your body's flexibility. Experience your body able to bend and move and stretch and turn with great ease. Feel how effortless it is to move your torso, your pelvis, your neck, your spine, your arms, your legs.

Experience yourself bending forward with ease, bending backward with ease, stretching to your right, stretching to your left. Experience your spine as being totally limber, totally healthy, totally flexible. Feel your body's flexibility.

6. Experience your body's grace. Experience your body flowing easily through space. Experience your body's complete ease of movement. Feel yourself as a dancer, moving through space with total grace and ease, barely touching the ground. Feel your body blowing through space as a breeze, totally fluid, totally graceful. Feel your body's flowing grace.

7. Experience your body's lightness, its buoyancy. Experience yourself floating on a cloud. Feel yourself totally weightless. Experience your body as completely buoyant in space, a feather floating in the wind. Experience your body as being totally light.

8. Experience your body's muscle tone. See your muscles perfectly toned, perfectly healthy, vibrant with aliveness. Experience this quality of vibrancy in each muscle of your body. Feel this vitality extending deep into each muscle. Feel your muscles toned to their highest level. Experience this feeling going right into the smallest muscle fiber.

9. Experience the purity of the muscle and bone tissue that composes your body. Experience how healthy your skin feels and looks. Experience how good it feels to have a body of such high-quality substance. Feel your physical purity. Feel this purity in every cell in your body.

10. Experience your body's absolute health. Feel your body as perfectly healthy, optimally healthy. Experience the sensation and feeling of total and absolute health. Allow this feeling to extend through every cell of your body. Allow it to permeate through every organ and every fiber of your being. Allow yourself to experience absolute and total health.

11. Experience your body as divinely beautiful. See yourself totally reflecting the highest beauty that exists in the universe. Feel yourself filled with this beauty. Radiate this inner beauty through your physical body. Experience yourself as the perfect reflection of all the beauty of the creation. Experience your physical beauty.

12. Experience your body's optimal physical well-being. See yourself at the pinnacle of human physical wellness. Feel and radiate your complete and total beauty. Experience and radiate your total and optimal health. Feel your complete gracefulness. Sense your purity, buoyancy, and lightness. Be vibrant with strength and endurance. Experience your boundless, unending energy and vitality. Experience all that is available to you as you drink deeply of the wonder of your body. Breathe this vision into your body.

Allow it to penetrate deep, deep, deep into the cells. Allow it to become part of the memory of each cell of your body.

13. Holding your vision of this optimal state of well-being, begin seeing your body shaped exactly as you want it to be. Do you want a certain part firmer, more toned? See it toned and firm. Do you want a part of your body to have more definition? See it with definition. Do you want to change the shape of your thighs or buttocks or stomach? See them the way you want them.

See your body exactly as you want it to look. The greater the clarity and definition of your vision, the easier this image can begin to manifest. How much does your ideal body weigh? How does it feel? Breathe this image into your body. Allow it to penetrate right into the memory of each cell. Allow it to become one with your core body essence. Breathe it in deeply, fully, totally.

14. Add anything else you need to make your vision complete. What else do you need to achieve optimum physical well-being? Refine your vision by adding whatever else your body needs in order to feel complete. Ask your body if there's anything else you should add to your vision.

15. Begin to experience this body you have created for yourself. In the body you have just envisioned, see yourself moving around the room. How do you move? How does it feel to be in this body? What can it do? Just notice and enjoy it for a while.

16. Now that you've enjoyed this body in your imagination, it's time to embody your vision. Get up from your chair or the floor and step into the body you have visualized. Experience this body as if you were entering into it for the very first time, as if this were your first experience of being in a body, as if you were "test driving" it for the first time.

How does it feel to be in this body? What can it do? How does it move? How does it bend? What kind of sensations does it experience? Experiment with it as you move. Make big moves. Make little moves. Delight in its pure physicality. Spend about five minutes in your renewed body. Let *it* tell *you* what to do with it. Move it to the music. Delight in it!

17. Bring your movements in your new body to a point of completion. Find your journal and record all that you experienced. How did it feel? How did this new body move? What could it do? Capture and record your experience of being in your visionary body. Allow the feeling of it to be present as you are writing. Allow your body to write through you.

Some comments people have made after doing this exercise include:

"I found this exercise so moving! It encouraged me to claim my new body as my birthright, because it *is* mine. I feel stronger. I feel lighter."

"I've always taken my body very much for granted. I've ignored it. It has done what I wanted it to do. It has placed very few restrictions on me. When I've damaged it, it has healed up. I really ignored it. This visualization had a liturgical quality to it. What it kicked off was the realization that my body, and all our bodies, are God's creation—and that means that I have something very special at my disposal."

"I feel alive, ecstatic, expanded, graceful, whole, joyous, free, wondrous, liberated, healthy, better than I've ever felt in my life, aware of my body like never before, in touch with my life energy, my power, my passion, and vitality."

This exercise was an opportunity to open up to what's possible for your body, to get in touch with its poetry and music. Through it you've begun a process of consciously creating your body as you want it. This implies taking responsibility for your body at the most profound level—its creation! This is no small act, and it's extraordinarily empowering. You've stepped into the driver's seat and taken charge. You aren't handing responsibility over to little invisible germs or family history or genetics. Yes, there are certain limits to your reimaging. You can't add six inches to your height or grow another limb, but your general health, physical condition, and body shape are totally within your control.

Your body will respond to the vision you hold for it. To make your current vision a reality you need to feel it deeply in your body, right at the cellular level. Your thoughts create your whole physical reality—your body is not exempt from this law.

Shortly after doing this exercise a workshop participant named Jim went to Jamaica on a holiday. He noticed all the strong, vital, healthy male bodies. He watched how they walked, how they danced, how healthy they looked, how strong and limber they were. He realized how few male bodies he had seen in America that were alive and inspiring to him. He realized just how impoverished his vision of a healthy male body had been. Jim fortified himself with these rich images.

On his return home he integrated what he had seen in Jamaica with what he had experienced in the body visioning exercise. Jim's vision for his own body was now very clear in his mind. He began a program to create his body as he wanted it. He started eating healthy foods, exercising, and feeling good about his body. Each day he renewed his vision. In less than a year he created his body exactly as he had envisioned it. He worked from the inside out.

The formula is very straightforward: We create a compelling vision of how we want our bodies to be and use that as the impetus to develop a program to create it. Let's look at how to create a program that will allow you to manifest your vision.

A Program for Body Well-Being

This program lays out the six building blocks for creating a healthy, vibrant, and fit body. After familiarizing yourself with each of these areas we encourage you to follow up with further reading, take classes, and, of course, follow your program consistently. The reading list we have at the back of this book will be helpful for your follow-up.

All of these elements of body well-being can be attained by just about anyone with a body. So if you have one, as seems likely, you're off to a great start! If you commit to each of these, your body should serve you well. If you're already doing some or all of these, acknowledge yourself and begin aligning your program with your body vision.

- **Stamina** In order to dance, if not all day and all night at least for longer periods of time, you need stamina. You develop stamina by exercising your heart and lungs, otherwise known as your cardiovascular system. Running, biking, rowing, fast walking, swimming, cross-country skiing, and of course dancing all build up endurance. There is a wide variety of resources available to you, places and people from whom you can learn about developing stamina. Our reading list includes several books we've found helpful. Start, of course, by consulting with your doctor.

- **Upper-body strength** Why do you need strength in your upper body to be in good physical condition? The answer is simple. You need to use your arms, back, stomach, abdomen, and chest all the time. Also, by developing your upper-body strength you develop a feeling of greater body confidence. You know that if you need it, the strength is there.

  Some of the ways to develop strength in your arms, chest, and upper back include: exercise machines, free weights, pull-ups, push-ups, and isometrics; for your lower back, stomach, and abdomen: sit-ups, leg raises, exercise machines, and free weights.

- **Flexibility** Can you bend your body easily or do you find yourself stiff? Suppleness should be a basic attribute of everyone's body. Yet unless you do exercises to keep your body flexible, it will stiffen up. Aside from this practical reason for developing flexibility, there is also an aesthetic reason: The more supple your body, the easier to elevate your movement to the grace of dance.

A good system to develop flexibility and suppleness in your body is hatha yoga.

• **Body Alignment** This element of body well-being is often overlooked, yet we believe it is essential to the proper mechanical functioning of the body. If the structural foundation is not right, everything else gets thrown off.

A car gets out of alignment from bumps in the road and similar shocks to its structure. This causes it to become unstable and begin veering to the right or left. The driver then must compensate by holding the steering wheel tight or turning the wheel a little bit more in the opposite direction. Our bodies, too, get knocked out of alignment through physical jars and ordinary day-to-day activities. This is compounded by negative emotions and mental stress, which create physical tension that tightens and shortens our connective tissue, causing even more structural imbalance. As the body is forced farther and farther out of alignment, we unconsciously compensate by putting stress on other muscles and soon grow accustomed to the imbalance.

We can function in this structurally imbalanced state. The question is, how much better could we function if we were aligned? Along with the more well-known chiropractic and osteopathic ways of creating alignment, there are a large number of bodywork systems that have emerged over the last fifteen years. Explore what's available and choose one that suits your needs.

• **Nutrition** The old saying "You are what you eat" is a truism. Your body is built up from the food you ingest. What kind of foods are you putting into it? We have a whole lifetime to live in just one body. We can't throw it away or trade it in when it starts to have problems. Therefore the food that we create it with is vital to its present and future well-being.

All the exercise in the world is of limited value if the actual body being exercised is made of junky materials. It's just a matter of time before we must pay the price for using inferior building materials. Food with no nutritional value, stuffed with preservatives, robs our body of its vitality and life energy. Fresh vegetables, fruits, nuts, and whole grains are living foods that add vitality to our bodies. It is possible to keep our bodies functioning on the processed, refined foods available today. But on such a diet there's no way that we can experience the heightened physical well-being brought by more natural foods.

Combining a natural and moderate diet with a sound physical regimen of aerobic exercise, upper-body strength, flexibility, body alignment, and a good daily dose of sunshine will give you the building blocks necessary for an elevated state of physical well-being. You deserve to have a body that exudes vitality, aliveness, and beauty. It is your birthright to have a body that feels good to be in, looks good, and performs at its optimum.

There is one final building block, however, that's essential in making all this come together. As you might guess, it's your mental attitude.

• **Mental Attitude** When you look at yourself in the mirror, what thoughts come to your mind? Do you say to yourself, "Wow, I sure am beautiful and healthy." Or do you say to yourself, "I don't like this part. I wish my body was more so-and-so," "I'm too fat," "I'm too this or that." Do you affirm your body or do you negate it?

What we think about our bodies goes right back into the cells and begins to manifest. The thoughts we think about our body are constantly creating it. The metaphysical corollary to the statement "We are what we eat" is "We are what we think." If you think negative thoughts about your body, it starts becoming duller and loses vitality. If we think positive thoughts about it, it starts becoming radiant and gains vitality. Our thoughts create our reality. Our body, albeit the densest part of our reality, is just one more part of it.

One great time to tell your body how much you love and appreciate it is while drying off after a shower or bath. As you rub the towel over your body tell it how much you appreciate and value it. Tell it how much you love it. It will respond. Another good time is when you look in the mirror first thing in the morning—it's a great way to start off the day. Your body will definitely appreciate the attention, and you become the beneficiary of a healthy and loved body.

To get your body well-being program in gear, make up a schedule listing the different elements you're going to work on and the day and time you'll work on them. Your first step may be educating yourself rather than physically starting the program. Begin where you need to begin. Then follow the plan you write down consistently.

For some of you the inspiration of your body vision is enough to get you moving to the next level. For others there may be a sense of being overwhelmed or a feeling of immobility that is the result of years of nonexistent or sporadic body care. If you're in the latter category, your first step needs to be transforming the beliefs that are holding you back. Let's take a look at some of the most common limiting beliefs that people face as they start caring for their bodies and at some turnaround affirmations that address these issues.

Common Limiting Beliefs and Turnaround Affirmations

LIMITING BELIEF: It's boring and too much trouble to care for my body.
TURNAROUND: I create a dynamic, sensual, outrageously fun body well-being program.

LIMITING BELIEF: I'm too busy doing other things to take care of my body.
TURNAROUND: My body is what allows me to do other things. I'm smart enough to put my priorities in the right order.

LIMITING BELIEF: I don't like my body and I can't change this attitude.
TURNAROUND: I've changed my attitude about other parts of myself, and I choose to change my attitude about my body. My body, I love you!

LIMITING BELIEF: I don't believe that I can make changes in my body—it's too far gone.
TURNAROUND: I take one step at a time. My first step is becoming friends with my body.

LIMITING BELIEF: I haven't taken care of my body in years. I feel overwhelmed and don't know where to begin.
TURNAROUND: I build a support system of people who help me begin the process of caring for my body.

LIMITING BELIEF: I hate all forms of exercise. I simply never exercise.
TURNAROUND: I reframe the experience of exercise to that of lyrical movement through which I joyfully take my body.

LIMITING BELIEF: I'm not a body person. I just can't get into taking care of it.
TURNAROUND: I engage my mind, heart, and spirit to create a partnership with my body, and together we explore a new way of being together.

LIMITING BELIEF: Unless I look like a *Vogue* model I won't be able to love my body.
TURNAROUND: I find my truth, am my own model, and love my unique one-of-a-kind body.

LIMITING BELIEF: I'm always tired and don't have enough physical energy.
TURNAROUND: I take responsibility to think energizing thoughts. My first thought is "The infinite energy of the universe flows through me."

LIMITING BELIEF: My body is not healthy and it will never be.
TURNAROUND: I take responsibility to heal my negative beliefs about the health of my body. I experience my body as radiantly healthy.

LIMITING BELIEF: I'll never achieve my ideal weight.
TURNAROUND: My body becomes what I visualize. I have a clear vision of how I want my body to be and I energize it every day. I am my ideal weight.

LIMITING BELIEF: I don't have enough discipline to follow through on an exercise or weight-reduction program.
TURNAROUND: I work from the inside out. I daily reconnect with my vision, and the discipline naturally and easily follows.

Perhaps one or more of these limiting beliefs helped you better understand a belief you're working with. If so, the turnaround affirmation should, with some personalizing, be able to serve as a foundation for your affirmation. It's now time to put all this information and self-discovery to work.

Creating an Affirmation and Visualization on Your Body's Growing Edge

What is the next step you can take to achieve the body you want? You have created a body vision. What affirmation and visualization will allow that vision to manifest? Perhaps it's an outer step like taking an aerobics class or going to a nutritional counselor. Perhaps it's an inner step like changing a major limiting belief. Here are the stories of several people who took our Empowerment Workshop and how they handled their body issues.

Bob's story demonstrates the need for time and patience when working on a major change in life. When Bob attended the Empowerment Workshop he was, by his estimate, a hundred pounds overweight. Though many other parts of his life were working well, he felt overwhelmed and hopeless when it came to his body. He didn't know where to begin.

Though he had lots of resistance to doing the body dialogue and body vision exercises, he stayed with the process and did the best he could. When the time came to create his affirmation Bob felt like he "should" make a statement about losing weight and exercising regularly. He tried out an affirmation but it had absolutely no feeling of vitality or possibility. He realized he was way ahead of his true growing edge. When he reread the dialogue with his body he had recorded in his journal, he realized his real growing edge for his body was acknowledging the need for and developing a positive support system and educating himself. He crafted the affirmation, "I have an active support system that facilitates the transformation of my wonderful body." His visualization was a support system that included a doctor, nutritionist, therapist, and body worker, all lovingly supporting and educating him.

Over the next year Bob created his wellness support network. In addition to medical and therapeutic support, he also joined Overeaters Anonymous and an Empowerment support group. His affirmations continued to serve as a foundation for the gradual changes he was making. Each time Bob became aware of his next growing edge he created an affirmation that represented the growth he wanted to see. "I am aware of what I eat;" "I celebrate my body and grow with the lessons it teaches me;" "I celebrate my self-love with my daily schedule, nourishing my body with exercise, meditation, and good food."

About a year and a half later Bob had lost fifty pounds. He decided to do the Empowerment Workshop a second time in order to revitalize all his growing edges and especially to take the work he'd been doing on his body to the next level. At this workshop he created an affirmation and visualization that addressed his next growing edge: "I choose to experience my body's full potential, and I commit to exercising for twenty minutes each day." His visualization was bicycling, flying with the wind, and laughing with friends. He committed to his program, lost the second fifty pounds—and began taking swing and ballroom dancing lessons!

Bob's story is important for several reasons. Any major change we make, be it in our bodies, in our relationships, work, or spirituality, requires us to stick with our process. A quote from Bob's journal indicates the patience he needed to stay with his growth process: "In all of these attempts to change and care for my body, I had successes and setbacks. With each of the affirmations I worked with, I learned something more about taking care of my body. Through it all I was learning to be patient and gentle with myself and to keep a positive attitude toward my body."

His statement could apply to any major change we wish to make in life. It is also important to note how Bob continually updated his affirmations as his growing edges evolved.

Rebecca's story is very different from Bob's. She came to the workshop with a wonderful, loving relationship with her body. Rebecca was running three to four miles every other day and had a body well-being program that integrated the six elements.

During the guided visualization on her body vision Rebecca had a breakthrough. As she mentally stepped into her new body she had an image and a distinct physical sensation of running the New York City Marathon. She had a feeling of extending her limits not just physically but emotionally and spiritually as well. She felt the marathon represented a rite of passage into deeper self-esteem. It was a symbol of owning her full power in the world. Developing her potential to run the marathon was a metaphor for developing her overall potential in life.

With great excitement she shared with other members of the group her insight and commitment to run a marathon. She crafted the affirmation and visualization, "I own my full power as I prepare for and complete my rite of passage—the New York City Marathon." Her visualization was crossing the finish line at Tavern on the Green in Central Park. After the marathon Rebecca wrote and said, "Not only did I complete the marathon, I completed my rite of passage." She had empowered herself to step more fully into her life. Just recently she fulfilled her lifelong dream of starting her own business.

Now let's look at Edward's story. Edward is one of those people who lives a fast-paced life and doesn't have time to deal with his body. He wasn't in any kind of pain, was just slightly overweight, and had enough energy. His body seemed to get by all right, and he didn't feel it warranted a lot of attention.

During the body dialogue Edward's body poignantly told him, "I faithfully get you around every day, yet you never thank me or acknowledge me. I feel unvalued and unloved. Please take the time to care for me. I can't keep going without attention!" Edward was quite touched by this and he knew it was true.

During the body visioning exercise he had an experience of how he would feel if he really took care of his body. In his body vision he felt strong, vibrant, and lean. He saw himself as being mentally and emotionally clear, more alive and energetic than he had ever been before. He realized how much of his overall aliveness he had missed by not taking care of his body. From this self-discovery Edward created the affirmation, "I am totally alive and generously love and care for my body through a program of exercise, nutrition, and relaxation." His visualization was the radiantly healthy body he had envisioned. Within six months Edward was enjoying living in that body.

The final story we'll share shows the range of what's possible with the affirmation visualization process. We'll let Laurie tell her story in her own words:

"I was four months pregnant and had been experiencing severe migraine headaches several times a week for most of that time. I was nervous about attending the workshop, certain I would spend at least some of that time bedded down somewhere with an ice pack on my head. During these four months I had tried acupuncture, vitamin therapy, and chiropractic adjustments—nothing really seemed to help.

"The first day of the workshop I came to understand I had a lot of fear about this pregnancy—mostly I was worried that something might be wrong with my baby and that no matter how well I took care of myself, it would not be enough. Just becoming aware of this was profound for me. I came up with this affirmation: 'I trust the way I am taking care of my body at this time, and my baby is healthy and happy.' To go along with this I had a visualization in my mind of a small, round baby in my womb with a kind of sappy smile on his face.

"For the rest of the pregnancy I repeated this affirmation to myself and visualized the image at the same time. I did this several times a day. I was headache free for the rest of the nine months, and my new little son smiled the same sappy smile many times during his infancy."

EXERCISE ▨▨▨▨▨▨▨▨▨▨▨▨▨▨▨▨▨▨▨▨▨▨▨▨▨▨▨▨▨▨▨

Body Affirmation and Visualization

It's now time to create your affirmation and visualization. Go back and review your body dialogue, your body vision, and the limiting beliefs and affirmations. Synthesize what you have learned and ask yourself, "What is the most important next step in caring for my body? What is my body growing edge?" Then, from the insight you have generated, create your affirmation and visualization.

Enjoy the gift of your body!

9

Money

"If you focus your attention on the lack of money, that's what will get reinforced. Where you put your mental attention is what gets nourished. Poverty comes to the person who is emotionally and intellectually prepared for it. Prosperity is attracted to the person who is emotionally and intellectually ready to accept it, expect it, and enjoy it."
                                                              —Jerry Gilles

T his quote says about money what we've been saying about every other area of life: Whatever we direct our mental attention toward, we create. Metaphysics, when applied to money, just happens to give us more tangible and quantifiable feedback. Do you focus your mental awareness on abundance and prosperity—or do you place it on lack and limitation? Do you believe that you will be prosperous—or do you believe you will always have to scrimp to get by? Your present financial situation is a direct reflection of what you believe about money and what you believe about your ability to create it. Your present reality concerning money can be traced back very clearly to specific beliefs you hold. What are those beliefs? This is where we will start our journey.

Your Beliefs About Money

We live in a materially oriented culture and, for better or worse, money is the symbol of this culture. It has a lot of power in our society and demands that we become clear about it. Blindly pursuing it as a god is not the answer, nor is denying it the answer.

Each of us needs to look carefully and honestly at the role money plays in our life. We need to sift through the different beliefs that we have been given by our parents, our peers, our religion, our society. We need to sort through our priorities and come up with our own truth for the material life-style we want. In doing this sorting we need to be particularly attentive to three areas in which we all receive a lot of programming.

• **Abundance vs. Scarcity** The two most common beliefs about money are that there's not enough of it—the fear of scarcity—and that you're not good enough or capable enough to have or deserve it—the denial of your creative potential. These two beliefs are so prevalent in our society, they have come to be labeled "poverty consciousness." The opposite of poverty consciousness is *prosperity consciousness: the belief in an abundant universe and your ability to fully partake of it.* It involves a trust that there will always be enough money to meet your needs and a confidence that you can easily create more when you need it. In the past, this idea might have been difficult to accept since most prosperity came from personal will applied to the manufacturing and exploiting of a limited amount of natural resources. Today, much prosperity comes from information which is a combination of intelligence, creativity, and personal will—all of which are unlimited.

• **More Is Better vs. Less Is Better** You can determine how much money is right for you by asking yourself, "What will allow me to be satisfied and to learn the lessons I'm here to learn?" For one person, becoming skillful in manifesting money and becoming a millionaire will most support his or her evolution. For someone with other lessons to learn, money may not be an important part of the curriculum. Each of us has his or her own classrooms; we have learned not to judge people by how much or how little money they have. The key, as in every other part of life, is that you are the creator of your reality. *No one but you can decide the right amount of money for you.*

• **Money Is Good vs. Money Is Bad** Many people believe that money is unspiritual and so they avoid it. But *money is neither good nor bad—it's neutral.* We refer to it as energy. It's our own inner state of consciousness that imbues this energy with destructive and manipulative power—or with healing and transformative power. It can be used to develop ourselves and to develop our society. For the world to evolve for the better, we need more people who are willing to enter into the arena of money and begin using this very powerful energy for good.

Most of the beliefs you hold about money are unconscious and unexamined. When you start bringing them to the surface, they may seem to be existential reality and not changeable. Nevertheless, if you want to change them, you can. First you must identify them—then you can change them. This next exercise provides you with an opportunity to do this.

Money—Limiting Beliefs and Turnarounds

As we said earlier, a limiting belief is like a weed in the garden. Unless you've cultivated your mental garden, it will have picked up weeds. Let's look at some of the major limiting beliefs about money and ways to turn them around. As you may recall, a turnaround statement is a new, expanded belief that reinterprets the way you view that aspect of reality. The turnaround process is a way of freeing up your thinking to be more creative, allowing you to see things from a wider vantage point. Many of these turnarounds below have come from participants in the Empowerment Workshop.

LIMITING BELIEF: Money is the root of all evil.
TURNAROUND: Money is neutral energy. It is my consciousness that imbues it with its power. I choose to imbue my money with healing and transformative power for me and the world.

LIMITING BELIEF: Money isn't spritual.
TURNAROUND: Money allows me to manifest my spiritual ideas and visions.

LIMITING BELIEF: Money will corrupt me.
TURNAROUND: I need to have spiritual development to take on the responsibility of having and working with money consciously. I commit to my spiritual development.

LIMITING BELIEF: Managing my money is uncomfortable and time consuming.
TURNAROUND: Managing my money is the means to channel and direct its power and energy consciously. I take responsibility for managing the energy I create.

LIMITING BELIEF: People won't like me if I have money.
TURNAROUND: Everyone has the potential to create prosperity. I am not intimidated by those who haven't claimed their power yet.

LIMITING BELIEF: I will lose all my friends when I become a millionaire.
TURNAROUND: All my friends are millionaires.

LIMITING BELIEF: Let's be honest and realistic: I'm not capable of earning the money I want.
TURNAROUND: I have successfully changed other parts of my life, I will successfully change this part as well.

LIMITING BELIEF: I have to struggle to create money.
TURNAROUND: I allow money to flow effortlessly into my life.

LIMITING BELIEF: There is a limited amount of money in the world, not enough to go around with millions suffering. If I have money, it means others won't.
TURNAROUND: There is as much money as there is energy to create value in the world. I harness my energy and create financial abundance as an act of self-love and as an example to others. I use my financial abundance to help myself and to help others.

LIMITING BELIEF: If I make a lot of money, I will become obsessed and out of balance.
TURNAROUND: I balance my material well-being with well-being in all the other parts of my life.

LIMITING BELIEF: I can't trust myself to use money wisely.
TURNAROUND: I define "wise" in my own terms and use my money wisely.

LIMITING BELIEF: I have too easy an access to inherited money and don't feel I deserve it.
TURNAROUND: I accept the gift of abundance in my life and use it for my good and the good of others.

LIMITING BELIEF: My spouse earns the money, and I don't feel I have the right to spend it.
TURNAROUND: I contribute my energy to creating well-being in the other parts of our relationship, and we freely share in the fruits of our mutual creativity.

LIMITING BELIEF: Working to earn money requires that I subjugate the spiritual and creative aspects of my life.
TURNAROUND: I make earning money a creative and spiritual activity.

LIMITING BELIEF: Money will not solve all my problems.
TURNAROUND: I now have one less problem.

EXERCISE

Limiting Beliefs about Money

The limiting beliefs and turnaround affirmations above should have warmed you up. It's now time to go into your mental garden and do some weeding. This limiting-belief exercise is similar to the one you did for sexuality. First you identify your limiting beliefs, then you replace them with turnaround statements.

The primary purpose of this exercise is to mentally clear your limiting beliefs. Don't fret over getting the turnaround worded perfectly. Right now your job is to remove weeds; later you can get into planting.

As you start bringing your beliefs to the surface, you may discover that some are deep-rooted and tough to turn around—you will probably find some that ultimately have very little to do with money. By all means take advantage of some of the turnarounds listed above. If they don't directly address your issue, spend some time thinking about your most positive vision for this aspect of your relationship with money. If this still doesn't produce a turnaround, be gentle and patient with yourself—it will come in time. The process of collecting these beliefs has taken a whole lifetime; the process of removing them may take a little while!

Some of the most common places to look for weeds in your money garden are your attitudes about: abundance vs. scarcity; your ability to create prosperity; religious and spiritual programming; parents; the cultural belief system; male and female programming; spending patterns; the nature of money.

Allow twenty to thirty minutes to do this exercise. You will need your journal. Space has been left in case you don't have it handy.

Write down your limiting beliefs about money. Concentrate *just* on your limiting beliefs and do not think about their turnarounds. Number them as you go.

When you feel you have written down all the limiting beliefs you can find, start turning them around. Start with the ones that you regard as the most important to turn around. Don't worry if you can't turn them around perfectly, just do the best you can.

Creating a Vision and Plan for Financial Well-Being

Now that you have some clarity about what you believe about money, you're ready for the next step—creating a financial vision and setting up a plan for manifesting it. The issues you need to address are: How much money do you want? How much surplus do you need to feel secure? Who can support you in manifesting this vision? What is the next step you must take to manifest your financial vision?

Easy questions, right? As you consider these questions notice what feelings are coming up for you. For some, the thought of creating a financial vision using real numbers is scary. Some common fears are:

- I'm petrified to deal with numbers.
- I don't have the ability to increase my income.
- "If I go for what I want and I don't succeed, I'll be a failure, so I'd better not try.
- I don't know how to make money.

For others the prospect of taking control of the financial part of their lives is highly exciting and motivating.

During this exercise notice what you're feeling each moment. What beliefs are being triggered in you? Be attentive to your inner process—use it to further uncover your beliefs about you and money. You will learn volumes if you're attentive. If you discover that you have more mental clearing to do, write down your limiting beliefs and create turnaround statements. If questions about work come up, hold them for the next chapter. Your purpose for now is to clarify what material well-being looks like to you. With this clear you can then develop a strategy for manifesting it.

One way to decide how much money you want is by determining what things you want to spend it on in the next year. Things such as a home, nice furnishings, travel, nice clothes, self-development, children's education, health care, ability to contribute to or create activities that are making a better world, etc., might be on your list. You may also want to create enough money so that you can take time to do non-income-producing activities such as retreats, extended travel, service projects, and artistic creation. Money can represent free time for self-development and social development. This is one of our favorite uses for our money. It's a reverse of the old saying "Time is money." In this case, money is time.

To come up with the dollar amount you want one year from today, you must work from your present sources of income. However, don't be afraid to be a little daring and adventurous with the number you choose. As we noted in the manifestation section of this book, the universe operates in unseen and mysterious ways. As soon as we believe in our vision we find ourselves attracting the worldly "nutrients" we need to manifest it. Money comes to us in ways that we could never imagine or dream up.

Jill was a banker with a fixed salary. She did this exercise and decided to really stretch. She didn't know where the money would come from, but she affirmed that it would come. At the end of the year there was a change in her bank's bonus policy, and bonuses were awarded strictly on merit. Jill was determined to be the most worthy and received 80 percent of the money in the pool. With this extra bonus she received exactly what she had been affirming.

A similar situation occurred for Alan. He ran a rock and mineral retail store and affirmed and visualized that his sales would double in the next month. He put his full intention and belief behind what he was affirming. Suddenly, expensive crystals that had just been lying around his store collecting dust started selling. At the end of the month he counted up the totals and discovered that his sales had doubled.

Because money is such a quantifiable area of life, the manifestation process is most obvious here. It doesn't work any more powerfully here than in other parts of life, it's just more recognizable. We have many letters from people who did our workshop, opened up their vision of what they thought was possible for them financially, and manifested what they affirmed. Anyone willing to clear away their limiting beliefs and believe in their financial vision will set the internal and external forces in motion to manifest it. The key idea here is to *clear your limiting beliefs and believe firmly in your vision*. Everything unfolds from this foundation.

Now, fill in the following blank:

One year from now I have a minimum annual income or net worth of $_____.

If you are creating your financial vision for five years from today, the prospects of what's possible open up dramatically. If you come up with a new business idea in the Chapter Ten, "Work," within five years it could be phenomenally successful. To get a new business up and running takes approximately two to three years.

The next question asks you to think about your long-term vision for material well-being. Having a clear vision will help you considerably in deciding how to invest your energy over the next five years. It's important to recognize that *committing yourself to creating a lot of money means committing yourself to investing a lot of your energy in income-producing activity*. Money returns to you as a result of the investment of your energy. It is the crystallization of your physical, mental, and psychic energy. If you do decide to create financial prosperity, the metaphysical knowledge and tools you have will assist you greatly.

I have a minimum income or net worth of $_____ in five years.

Inherent in the idea of investment is surplus. It means you have generated more money than you need for your basic needs. Developing surplus income is like a farmer building a grain bin. The farmer expects a surplus and plans for it. If the farmer does not plan for surplus, he or she will not harvest beyond his or her basic needs. It's the same with us: *If we don't have a plan for how we will use money beyond our basic needs, we won't expend our energy beyond that point.* We unconsciously stop the flow of our psychic and mental energy when we reach the limit of our vision. If our vision is just enough money to get by, that's what we create. If our vision is one of surplus, then that's what we create. Our thoughts create our reality, a story you should know by heart by now.

One of the most graphic examples of this phenomenon of generating just the amount of money you expect and no more is in the field of sales. It is well known in the sales industry that salespeople sell just enough to meet the goal they set for themselves. They pace the output of their mental and psychic energy to create the amount of money they expect. The key is expectation.

Once you decide you're going to create surplus, you need to determine a definite amount that you want and a definite place to put it. To come up with this amount, ask yourself, "How much money beyond my basic needs do I require in order to feel secure?" One equation people find helpful is to have at least enough to cover their basic needs for six months in case they get ill. Beyond a minimal surplus, what amount would give you the most security? If you doubt your ability to manifest money, you might need a lot of money to feel secure. If you feel very confident of your money-making abilities and have a high degree of trust, you may feel secure with considerably less.

After you have come up with a number that represents how much, then you need to decide where you will invest this money. The most secure investments provide a modest and safe rate of return. If you want to invest more speculatively, make sure that the money you use for this is above and beyond what you need to feel secure. Then carefully educate yourself and seek advice from a competent financial advisor.

It's also important to recognize that your surplus money is your surplus energy. Where it gets invested is a personal statement about what you want to support with your energy. Today, many people are putting their money in money market funds that invest in socially responsible businesses. These money market funds are producing comparable and, in some cases, better yields than ordinary money market funds. Consider carefully what your money is being used for when you're deciding where to invest it.

Now, fill in the following blank:

Three years from today I have created a surplus of $_____.

The better your personal growth support system, the more you enhance your capacity to grow. Likewise, the better your prosperity support system, the more you enhance your capacity to grow financially. To create a prosperity support system you need to ask yourself the question "Who can enhance my ability to be more prosperous?" Some of the kinds of people you should consider including are: people you know directly or indirectly who are prosperous, a financial advisor, an accountant, people who can help you work with your beliefs about money, clients and prospective clients, and people in your field who are financially successful. *The primary criterion for selecting these people is that they can support you in becoming prosperous and successful, either by example, advice, or future business.*

If you are seeking someone to act as a role model, approach people who could serve this purpose for you. Tell them your intention is to learn what allowed them to become prosperous and successful. In most cases they will be quite cooperative, honored to be held in such esteem by you. As you listen to them tell their stories, always keep in mind your own unique truth. You are seeking to cull their wisdom and apply it to your personal style and way of being in the world. You are not attempting to become copies of them.

My life is filled with _____, people who are helping me become prosperous and successful.

You've set your sights on how much money you want to create and who can help you. What is the next step you need to take to translate your vision into action? It may be to seek out a financial advisor who can help you more fully develop your financial options. It may be to assess how what you are presently doing can generate more money. Perhaps you can increase your number of clients, become more entrepreneurial, raise your fees, ask for a raise, or start another business on the side. If your next action is work-related, you will be well primed for the next chapter.

Take time to consider the next action you will take. Let this action provide the momentum to generate the next action, and so forth. The journey of a thousand miles begins with the first step. Let your first step on the path to abundance be one that begins making your goal real to you.

To manifest my financial vision my next action step is _____.

Creating an Affirmation and Visualization on Your Money Growing Edge

What is your growing edge for money? Maybe it's to work on a particularly challenging limiting belief. Perhaps it's to further develop some part of the work you did on your financial vision and plan. To help you determine your growing edge we'll share some stories of how other people worked on their money growing edge.

*   *   *

Chris was constantly struggling with money; he knew this would be an important part of the empowerment journey for him. As he did the limiting-belief exercise he was astonished at how many deeply felt limiting beliefs he found. They all seemed to boil down to the idea that there just wasn't enough and so he'd better hold on to what he had. He came to realize that his poverty consciousness had a profound impact on how he lived his life. He kept a job he didn't really like because it was safe and secure; lived in a house he had long outgrown; never took a vacation because he needed to save the money. Chris realized that he was constantly holding back, afraid to live his life fully for fear that there wouldn't be enough. With this awareness came a lot of sadness and a yearning to change his attitude.

Chris understood that he needed to trust that there was an abundant universe in which he could participate. He crafted this affirmation and visualization: "I am abundant and live my life fully trusting in an abundant universe." His visualization was seeing himself in a beautiful house in the country. About a year after Chris created this affirmation and visualization, we received the following letter:

"Since I last saw you the most dramatic change in my life has come from changing my beliefs from scarcity to abundance. Over and over I have used my affirmation, 'I am abundant and live my life fully trusting in an abundant universe.' With this belief as my new friend, I have exceeded the projections in my financial plan and have made the following changes in my life. I resigned from my job of nine years and quickly thereafter received three job offers. One of them was exactly the kind of job I wanted, and it was double my former salary. I sold my home and bought a new home in exactly the place I had always wanted to live. I furnished it just as I had visualized it. Furthermore, between leaving my old job and taking my new one I took a six-week vacation. Thank you for helping me change my life!"

When people open up to living in abundance rather than the fear of lack, dramatic changes are set in motion.

Linda had absolutely no relationship to money. She struggled through the limiting-belief and turnaround exercise and was overwhelmed by the notion of creating a financial vision and plan. In her journal she tells her own story: "Dealing with money is earth-shattering for me. Having to think about it has touched such a raw nerve. I am intimidated and afraid of it. I have lived my whole life thinking I don't have to deal with money. It is not a reality for me. I have never thought of planning any kind of financial future for myself. It never occurred to me that I could have any control over this part of my life."

Linda decided that before she could create a financial vision, she needed to learn to think positively about money. Her affirmation was "I have a positive relationship with money and it empowers me." Her visualization was walking down a pathway lined on both sides by money trees, which increased in size and number the farther along she went. Linda found her growing edge in money and took the appropriate first step.

Larry was someone who financially just managed to get by. He believed that thinking about money was unspiritual, so he never thought about it and never had any. His insight after doing the limiting belief and turn-around was that desiring material well-being was healthy and a normal part of living in a material world. It was *as* important and not *more* important than caring for the emotional and spiritual parts of his life.

This was a breakthrough for Larry. He was excited as he worked on his financial plan and began to give positive energy to this ignored part of his life. He crafted this affirmation and visualization: "I generously nurture the money part of my life and create a materially and spiritually balanced life." In his visualization he was standing on a mountaintop basking in the radiant sunshine in his best hiking gear.

About a year and a half after he took the Empowerment Workshop he sent us a letter. He fulfilled the projections of his one-year financial prosperity plan, and as a result he was experiencing a newfound sense of self-confidence. In his own words, "With this deeper self-confidence I notice my work as a therapist is clearer and more transformative than ever, my relationship is more alive and growing, and we've just bought a dream house I wouldn't have even considered a year ago."

Beth was the mother of five children. Caring for her family was a full-time job, and she felt very good about her role as a mother and wife. However, when it came to money Beth felt confused and stuck. During the limiting belief and turnaround exercise she became aware of her belief that it was not okay to spend money on herself because she didn't earn it. Furthermore she believed she had to ask her husband, Jim, for permission whenever she wanted to spend money on the household and on the children.

As Beth worked on turnarounds for these limiting beliefs she was struck by the concept of money as green energy. She wrote this in her journal: "If money is green energy that means Jim generates the green energy in our family. I generate love, caring, support, and a healthy, nourishing home environment for Jim and our family. I generate the white energy in our family. We need both green and white energy in order to have a high-quality life. I know Jim feels he deserves the white energy that I generate, and he uses it freely. Yes! Of course I deserve the green energy he generates, and I can use it freely."

Her affirmation read, "I create an abundance of white energy and Jim creates an abundance of green energy; we share equally of these energies." Her visualization was great shafts of green and white light pouring forth and mingling together.

Beth learned that self-worth can be measured in many ways.

EXERCISE

Money Affirmation and Visualization

These stories demonstrate the range of issues people work on in this part of life. It's now time for you to address your growing edge and create your affirmation and visualization for money. Go back to your work on limiting beliefs and turnarounds and your plan for financial well being. Also remind yourself about the action step you wrote down earlier. Take this information and condense it into a succinct statement of the next place of growth in the area of money. Refine this statement to its essence and write your affirmation and visualization in your journal or in the space below.

10

Work

"When you work you fulfill a part of earth's furthest dream assigned to you when that dream was born, and in keeping with labour you are in truth loving life. And to love life through labour is to be intimate with life's inmost secret. And what is it to work with love? Is it to weave the cloth with threads drawn from your heart, even as if your beloved were to wear that cloth. It is to build a house with affection, even as if your beloved were to dwell in that house. It is to sow seeds with tenderness and reap the harvest with joy, even as if your beloved were to eat the fruit. It is to charge all things you fashion with a breath of your own spirit, and to know that all the blessed dead are standing about you and watching.

"Work is love made visible. And if you cannot work with love but only with distaste, it is better that you should leave your work and sit at the gate of the temple and take alms from those who work with joy. For if you bake bread with indifference, you bake a bitter bread that feeds but half man's hunger. And if you grudge the crushing of the grapes, your grudge distills a poison in the wine. And if you sing though as angels, and love not the singing, you muffle man's ears to the voices of the day and the voices of the night."

—Kahlil Gibran, The Prophet

What allows you to work with love? Love is manifest through work that is an expression of your inmost calling; work that is worthy of your highest effort; work that reflects your deepest caring for other people. It is your absolute right and privilege to experience work as the blessed gift it is meant to be.

To be truly fulfilled in your life you must do work that you love, work that enlivens you and brings forth your passion. To settle for anything less is to deny yourself one of life's great treasures. And the truth is that you *can* create your work the way you want it. With a clear vision, inspiration, and proper understanding of how to go about it, you can create your work exactly the way you want it.

There are generally five ways people view their work. See where you fit:

• **Fulfilled** You are already doing work that you experience as love made visible. You have created a work situation that is deeply fulfilling to your mind, heart, spirit, and body. It is challenging you to grow, both personally and professionally. You experience deep meaning in how you are using your life. For you there is no difference between work and play. Your work is your earthly playground. You are very blessed. The work vision for you revolves around how good it can get.

For you this chapter is an opportunity to push back the limits of what you consider possible in your present work.

• **Dissatisfied** You are clearly not doing work that is satisfying. Your work may not be challenging, or in alignment with your personal values, or giving you a sense of meaning. In your job working conditions may not be tolerable. For whatever the reason, your present work is not where you want to be.

This chapter will grant you a reprieve from a dissatisfied work life. It will give you an opportunity to envision and learn how to create the kind of work you would like.

• **Just Getting By** You neither like nor dislike your present work. You go to work each day, and although there's nothing offensive about your work, it doesn't excite you and engage your passion. Perhaps you've fallen into a rut and you don't face any challenges at work. Perhaps you are bored or burned out.

Sometimes, by making certain subtle but strategic shifts in your thinking, you can fall back in love with your work. You can create a work that reengages your passion. In this chapter we will look with you for those leverage points that can elevate the quality of your work experience.

• **A Stepping-stone** You do work that you know is not your final destination but is a stepping stone toward it. Work is providing you with training and experience in a field you will either stay in or which can be adapted to another similar field. You are learning a lot of practical skills and your work is fulfilling. You still face a learning curve.

You will have an opportunity in this chapter to make sure this step is still relevant, to sharpen your vision of where your path will ultimately lead, and to make sure you are getting the most out of your present situation.

• **Transition** You are between jobs and wide open to what's next. You may be searching for a new career in a field in which you have no experience or you may want to continue in your current field of work. Perhaps you need time to just be before you get back into work, or perhaps you're actively searching for your next job.

You are in an excellent position to start with a clean slate. You will be able to clarify your vision and make sure your next work experience is all that you want it to be.

Creating Your Ideal Vision for Work

To have your work be love made visible you need to love your work. The purpose of this next exercise is to create a vision for your work that represents what you would most love to do. Your vision may be a more fulfilling version of what you're already doing or it may be very different from your current work experience.

If you could create your work to be any way you wanted, what would it look like? If all your talents, gifts, imagination, creativity, and uniqueness were completely engaged, what would your work look like? If your mind, heart, body, and spirit were totally integrated, and this integration were fully expressed in your work, what would it look like? If your highest personal and social values were represented by your work, what would it look like? If who you are at the deepest level formed the core of your work, what would that work be? If someone gave you permission to do any kind of work on earth, regardless of prior training or experience, what would it be?

We can have our work be all that we can envision. But first we need a vision. With a clear vision, firm commitment, and the knowledge to bring it about, we embark on an odyssey to discover our full potential. This potential not only nourishes your soul, it nourishes your body. Michael Phillips, developer of MasterCard and author of *The Seven Laws of Money*, says:

> *The hardest thing to convince people of is a fact that only the very rich know. The way to make money is to do exactly what you want to do and do it exactly the way you want to do it. True, you have to make adjustments to marketplace realities as you go along, but the principal way to achieve wealth is to hew as closely as possible to your own inner vision. Only your own idea can fuel you with the energy and passion to continue during the inevitable early discouragements.*

During this exercise give yourself permission to let go of what you previously thought possible, your past experience and your past training, and allow your heart and passion to speak to you. The key is not to let the past weigh you down as you take flight. You can pick up your reasonableness, skills, and past experience again at the other end of this visioning exercise. In all likelihood you will find yourself building on them. As Jonathan Livingston Seagull once said, "The gull who flies highest, sees farthest." Enjoy the view!

EXERCISE

Ideal Work Vision

Allow approximately twenty minutes to do this exercise. You will need your journal and colored pens or drawing materials for drawing images. Space has been left in case you don't have your journal. Find a quiet place where you will be undisturbed. Sit in a comfortable chair and put on some quiet, relaxing music.

This guided visualization is divided into eight questions. After each question close your eyes so you can more easily connect with your imagination and creativity. When you're ready, with soft eyes, record or draw your response in your journal.

Take several deep breaths and allow yourself to connect with your visionary self. When you're ready, go to the first question.

1. In your ideal vision for your work, what does the environment look like? Are you indoors or outdoors? Are you in an office, your home, or somewhere else? What are the aesthetics and feeling of your environment? Is there any music or art or plants? What are the colors? If you're indoors, what do you see when you look out the window? Is the decor natural, modern, folksy, elegant? Describe your environment in as much detail as possible. You might want to draw a picture of what you envision.

2. In your ideal vision for work, what are you doing? Are you providing a service? Are you creating a product of some sort? Are you inventing something? What is the field of your endeavor: the arts, education, healing, public service, media, science, communication, sports, food, building, travel, crafts, finance, leisure activities, etc.? Describe or draw what you're doing.

3. In your ideal vision for your work, how do you structure it? Are you working on your own or with others? Are you managing others? Are you traveling? How many hours a day, or days a week, or weeks a year do you work? Is your workplace formal or informal? Do you own your own business or do you work for someone else? Describe or draw your structure.

4. In your ideal work, what are the values by which you operate: love, integrity, excellence, compassion, honesty, commitment to human potential, hard work, loyalty? Describe or illustrate all the values that are important to you in your ideal work.

5. In your highest vision for your work, what talents and gifts are you expressing? What are the challenges you have that allow you to grow, stretch, and fully express your unique talents and gifts? Describe or draw.

6. In your highest vision, how are you being acknowledged for your effort so that you feel valued? What do people tell you about your work? How much money are you receiving? Describe or draw.

7. In your highest vision for your work, describe the kind of people you are working with. Describe the quality of your communication with these people. Describe the effect your presence has on the people you work with.

8. Add anything you need to round out and make more complete your highest vision of how you would like your work to be.

Take a few moments to immerse yourself in the totality of the vision you have just created. Take a few deep breaths. How does it feel to experience your highest vision for your work? Allow this feeling into your body. Let it gently into your heart. Experience this feeling in your mind. Let it permeate your spirit. Allow yourself to fully own and accept your vision as something that is available to you.

After this exercise people are generally feeling quite excited. For you it may have been a revelation of a whole new way to think about expressing yourself in your work and life in general. It may have been a confirmation that you're already doing what you love and your only task is to tune up your vision. Some envision something they can start working on tomorrow; for others it will take some time. Perhaps you need more training or experience or time to reflect on what you discovered. You have as much time as you need. You now have a blueprint of what you want to build, and you can move as fast or as slowly as you desire. Trust your inner guidance as to the right pace for you.

A professor who did this exercise in the Empowerment Workshop wrote to us later with his story: "This experience opened up my intuitive sense of the world that has been so constrained in the academic world. My academic success has depended on linear thinking, and I believe I am very good at it. But I was afraid to guide it with my other dimensions, so I limited my insights, often not connecting with my sensing and intuition.

"Bringing the two together had the effect of—well, it feels like the two halves of my brain had been trying to reach each other, and the barriers were finally blown apart.

"The effect of this was to enable me to make connections between the many disparate areas of research and thinking that I have immersed myself in for years. I am an integrative thinker and had put many pieces of the puzzle together before. But the sections never joined. After the workshop they began to fly together as if magnetized—I could suddenly see the big picture. At this point I believe I am in a position to write what may be one of the most significant works in organizational and individual change."

One woman did not find a specific task but learned what the feeling would be like in her ideal workplace: "I asked myself the question, 'Who am I working with in my ideal workplace?' and the answer I got was 'My parents.' Looking around, I saw all kinds of other people working there too. But I just got this feeling that went through me, that this was my special place, that this was right. It was like electricity.

"I don't have a confident answer to the question of what I am going to go out and do, and yet, more and more images are coming to me of what my ideal work could be like. I'm just putting together the pieces, starting with what I know I want. For instance, I have so much love to give, and knowledge of the truth that life is easy and fun, that we can have it all. I know I can turn people on just by who I am in my work. In my ideal work environment I could perceive the state of the people around me. When I would reach out to them they turned from being really sad to being really happy. I'd like to do that on the subway or on a bus, to see how many people I can make smile.

"I'm less worried now about the form. I kept wondering what the form of my work would be, but for now I'm just concentrating on giving who I am."

Making Your Vision Real in the World

When we touch our innermost vision of how we want to express ourselves on this planet, we release our life energy. Our passion for living surges, making all that power available to bring this vision into form. Whether you are inspired to move slowly or quickly, there are seven essential ingredients to taking your passion and making it happen.

Making your passion happen requires a knowledge of how to be successful in the world of action—and a commitment to using this knowledge. In our experience we have seen these seven qualities demonstrated by people who are successful in making their love visible in their work. If you embody these seven qualities, it's just a matter of time before your highest dream for your work becomes a reality.

• **A *Success* Plan** It seems quite basic, and it is. The captain of an airplane has a flight plan. The captain of a ship has a navigational plan. A business owner has a business plan. A general has a battle plan. Without a plan these leaders have nothing to aid them in getting to where they want to go or accomplishing their goals. If you are to be successful in manifesting your vision for work, you need a success plan. You're already halfway there because you have a work vision that spells out what you want to create. Now you need to create a plan to move your vision forward the next step.

Go back to your eight answers and decide upon an action you can take to move each of the eight parts of your vision forward one step. Use the same creativity you used to come up with your vision to start manifesting it.

You don't need to figure out in detail how you'll get to your final destination, but you do need to start moving toward it. As you keep holding your vision clearly in your mind, you will begin attracting opportunities. The opportunities may appear as people who can help you, courses you can take, special projects at work that allow you to prove yourself. Knowing where you're going allows you to respond to these opportunities decisively. Keep this certainty in mind: Your vision is an accomplished fact, and your primary job is to have fun figuring out how you did it.

• **Self-confidence** People who are successful have confidence in their ability to achieve their goals. They project that confidence and it inspires other people to do business with them or trust in their capabilities. Although they may have their moments of doubt, their primary way of being is self-confident. They believe in themselves, their vision, and their ability to accomplish it.

The way we develop self-confidence is by going for something and accomplishing it. What we go for does not have to be a big thing. All that is necessary is that we stay with it until we achieve success. This is what breeds confidence in us and allows us to go for the next challenge.

To develop confidence that you can achieve your work vision, take your next action step in each of the eight areas of your vision. Each time you accomplish a step, acknowledge yourself and let that success give you confidence to walk further down the path.

• **Increase** People who are successful help others. They increase the well-being of others. They take the time to lend a hand or offer an encouraging word, and the fascinating thing is that as they help others succeed, they find themselves receiving exactly what they put out. What we put out, we get back.

A man we know ran a successful trade publication for the health-food industry. He was asked for information about the industry by a representative of a large New York magazine publishing company that was considering developing a competitive magazine. He told his future competitor how successful the industry was, who his major clients were, and other strategic business information. He also encouraged his competitor to enter the field, telling him how much it would improve the quality of the industry.

Ironically, he scared away his competitor, who decided that anybody who felt that confident and was that generous would be too formidable a competitor. Ultimately he became a major supporter of his business.

Wishing others success can work in many ways. It is a pure act that springs from the certainty of abundance. It is a statement that there's *enough*—on this planet, in my industry, in my profession. It's a belief that my wishing you success or helping you achieve it will in no way limit me from having success—it will actually contribute to my success. Who can you help succeed? Notice the opportunities that come along to be helpful. It will make you feel good and it will reap practical rewards in ways you can't anticipate.

● **Persistence**

> "Nothing in the world can take the place of persistence. Talent will not; nothing is more common than unsuccessful people with talent. Education will not; the world is full of educated derelicts. Persistence and determination alone are omnipotent. The slogan 'press on' has solved and always will solve problems of the human race."
> —Calvin Coolidge

Persistence is a refusal to give up and a commitment to continue firmly, steadily, and insistently.

The stories of the persistence of those who ultimately became successful are legend. Edison's multiple failures before he perfected the light bulb; the Beatles' many early rejections before they became popular; Abraham Lincoln's loss of almost every election in which he ran, yet still winning the presidency, etc. Those who succeed have a large store of persistence.

We have a friend who is in the fund-raising business. Extracting money from people is certainly one of the more challenging professions. To accomplish his goals he devised a very unusual technique. He had a sheet of paper with several hundred names and five columns next to each name. A day's work for him was going through his list of names until he reached fifty "no's." He also would keep calling an individual until he got five "no's" from that person. He literally did not take no for an answer. He defined the concept of no as a state of resistance, not the end of the process of interacting with the person. He ultimately was so successful that he became president of the company for which he used to do fund-raising.

If you want to succeed, you need to be willing to accept resistance as a natural part of the process. Most of us don't have to deal with the amount of resistance our fund-raiser friend encountered. Nonetheless, to accomplish your vision you will have to deal with and overcome much resistance. The more pioneering and entrepreneurial your vision, the more resistance you will encounter. If you are willing to stay with it, you will accomplish your vision for work. The secret for dealing with resistance is, don't focus on the resistance, focus on your vision. You will manifest your vision more quickly—and have fun doing it.

- **Intuition** We never have enough information to make a decision just on the facts. Cultivating and using your intuition—sometimes called your hunch, your gut, or inner guidance—is very important to your success. You need to be willing to trust what you feel and act on it.

Those who wait for what they are feeling to be proven before they act become historians. But if that's not your calling, you would be wise to develop your intuition as an aid to making decisions. One technique that is helpful in determining how to respond to your intuition is to see whether the thought of acting on it expands or contracts you. Does the action cause you to feel excited and open or fearful and closed? If it expands you, you are opening up to the flow of energy inside yourself and in the universe. If it contracts you, you are closing down to that flow of energy. Either response can be right depending on the situation. Your intuition might cause you to feel contracted because there is danger ahead or expanded because you have great potential for success ahead. The key is to be attentive to what you're feeling, then act on it.

- **Positive Presentation** At long last some acknowledgment of the superficial things in life! Positive presentation is how well your shoes are polished, the kind of suit you wear, the neatness of your business letter, your speech, your business card and letterhead. In the action arena we are judged by appearances. This is the first thing someone notices about you—and it tells a lot. It says you care about yourself and what others think about you. It says you pay attention to detail. It says you conduct yourself in a professional manner. It says you're capable of communicating your ideas. Often, all that people initially have to go on in deciding whether to give you their business or their confidence is your external presentation.

Charlie couldn't afford to buy new furniture for the waiting room of his new office. So he filled it with high-quality furniture from his home to give prospective clients the appearance of success. He knew that people wanted to feel secure in knowing that his business was not a fly-by-night operation.

Anne realized that to be promoted to management positions she had to be able to communicate her ideas more clearly. She started developing her vocabulary and communication skills.

Look at your vision and find the points where you interact with others.

What can you do to make sure that the presentation of what you do is as positive as can be?

● **Love** To have your work be love made visible you need to find ways to integrate love into your work practices. It won't be there unless you put it there. Love in the workplace is unfortunately quite uncommon. Most people are afraid to go beyond the very narrow boundaries of what they believe is acceptable. Yet everyone wants love and spends a great deal of energy seeking it out. If you incorporate it in your work, you will not only feel happier, but others will seek you out like a bee going to honey. An example of this is a woman who ran a restaurant with love.

Even though she was located in a poor section of town and her food was just okay, she still had lots of business. The reason was that she made a point of offering a heartfelt blessing to everyone who ate in her restaurant. She offered her customers more than nourishment for the body; she offered them nourishment for the heart. People were willing to overlook the food because her love for each person who walked into her restaurant was so strong. Eventually she was so successful that she was able to open a restaurant in a better location and hire a top-notch chef. She then made adding love to the menu her exclusive work.

In your business dealings, don't you prefer a person who is loving and kind over a person who is not? Who gets the larger tip, the person who serves you with a smile and love or the person who does not?

Along with the external rewards—more people wanting to take advantage of your product or service—you feel good. You end the day knowing that many people feel better because of you. These people reciprocate love and fill you up even more. Look through your work vision and find all the places where you can add that secret ingredient of love to the menu you offer to the world.

With a clear vision, grounded in concrete knowledge about manifesting it, you're on track. It's now time to create your affirmation and visualization for your growing edge in work.

To find out what your growing edge is, think back to the ideal work vision exercise you did earlier in this chapter. Were there any parts of your vision that were blank or seemed difficult? That exercise gave you a positive vision of what you want in your ideal work situation. How might one or more of the seven qualities assist you in manifesting this vision? Is there anything stopping you from getting there?

To assist you in clarifying your growing edge, we list some common limiting beliefs and turnaround statements below. We'll also share with you some stories of how others have worked with their growing edge for work. Use this input to create your affirmation and visualization for your work growing edge.

Creating Your Work Affirmation and Visualization

LIMITING BELIEF: It's not possible for me to do work I really like.
TURNAROUND: Lack of vision and a commitment to it is the only thing that can hold me back from doing work that I really enjoy. I create and manifest my work vision.

LIMITING BELIEF: I can never make enough money doing what I really enjoy.
TURNAROUND: The best way to make a lot of money is by doing something I not only enjoy but adore. I create work that expresses my creativity, passion, and full commitment.

LIMITING BELIEF: I love my work, but I'm always getting burned out.
TURNAROUND: I focus the emphasis of the work I do on people's potential, creativity, and growth. Being around this positive energy continuously regenerates me.

LIMITING BELIEF: I just don't have what it takes to be really successful in my work.
TURNAROUND: I have a vision and a plan for manifesting it. I'm already ahead of the majority of people I work with. Watch out, world!

LIMITING BELIEF: I can't have meaningful work that also pays well.
TURNAROUND: I use my creativity, ingenuity, and entrepreneurial instincts to create work that is both meaningful and financially rewarding.

LIMITING BELIEF: If I really love my work, I will become preoccupied with it and the rest of my life will suffer.
TURNAROUND: I love my work and the satisfaction it gives me and take responsibility to carefully balance it with the other parts of my life that I also love.

LIMITING BELIEF: I don't know how to ignite passion for work.
TURNAROUND: I use my creativity to turn what most excites my passion into my work.

LIMITING BELIEF: Even though I don't like my job very much, it pays me a good salary and I'm afraid I won't be able to do as well somewhere else.
TURNAROUND: I trust in my own creativity and the abundance of the universe to provide me with work that totally fulfills me. I act on this trust.

LIMITING BELIEF: Business is a dog-eat-dog world. I can't satisfy my humanistic needs in this environment.
TURNAROUND: If I believe that business is a dog-eat-dog world, that's

what I create it to be. I take responsibility to create a people-oriented, humane business environment.

LIMITING BELIEF: If I attempt to be loving and open in a business environment, people will laugh at me and call me flaky.
TURNAROUND: Business is made up of ordinary human beings who want to give and receive love but who are afraid that it's against the rules. I take responsibility to initiate communication that is open, vulnerable, kind, and loving and create my business environment as I want it to be.

When Kathleen did this exercise she held a secretarial job that, in her own words, was "pure drudgery." She had accepted the classical limiting belief that work is not to be enjoyed but endured. The idea that you could be in love with your work, that work could be love made visible, was completely new territory for Kathleen, and she was intrigued.

During the work vision exercise she allowed her imagination to soar and left her office job far behind. Her vision made it very clear that she yearned to be a potter. She had repressed this dream for a long time. Kathleen got goose bumps when she considered the possibility of actually fulfilling this dream! She recognized that her growing edge was to make a gentle transition over time from her current job to being a potter. With this in mind Kathleen crafted this affirmation and visualization: "I take the appropriate first steps to fulfill my dream of becoming a potter and support my learning and apprenticeship phase by income from my present job." In her visualization Kathleen saw herself selling her pottery at a crafts fair in the country with lots of people buying her pottery and appreciating her talent.

Slightly over a year later we received a package in the mail from Kathleen, with a beautiful large dish inside and letter attached. "I have been showing my work at craft shows and people are actually buying my pottery. Who would have ever thought? It's with great pride, joy, and gratitude that I send you this plate and ask you to be joyful with me!"

Gabrielle was quite dissatisfied with her job, and knew she needed to make some changes. We'll let her tell the story. "Work was a major issue for me when I took the Empowerment Workshop. I was in a management job which was out of control, frustrating, futile, and which assaulted my values and integrity daily. I needed an entirely new career, and I envisioned one for myself during the exercise on ideal work. I created this affirmation and visualization: 'The full power of my vision for work manifests within one year.' In my visualization, I saw and felt myself in the ideal vision I'd created. "About one and a half years later I was reviewing my work affirmation and visualization and realized that my successful new career was exactly how I had pictured it during the work visioning exercise. I was shocked how *exactly and completely* I had manifested my vision. Every element—each of the eight steps—I had described in my vision was contained in my new career! I had included in my initial vision flexible hours, travel, the type of groups who would be my clients, the pace and place of work, the teaching, guiding, advising, facilitating, growing components of the training and consulting career that I now enjoy!" Gabrielle knew what she wanted, had the courage to go for it, and created it all.

Susi was a young dynamo. When we met her she was in a job she knew was a stepping-stone. She clearly realized that her current job as assistant director of communications for a large sports-marketing company would give her the experience to one day start her own sports-marketing public relations company.

After doing the work vision exercise she realized that she had stopped growing in her job. She wasn't being challenged or learning new skills. She wasn't getting the training she wanted. She was getting lulled into complacency.

Susi decided to take the steps necessary to make her present job more challenging and growthful. She created this affirmation and visualization: "I increase my level of responsibility so that I have greater challenge and the opportunity to develop new skills." In her visualization she saw herself talking to her boss and proposing a broadened scope of work.

In a subsequent phone conversation with Susi we learned that she went to her boss and told her what she needed to be challenged and to grow professionally. Her response was to promote Susi to director of communications and redefine her own role now that Susi would be taking on a lot of her old responsibilities. Susi not only empowered herself to get what she wanted, she also empowered her boss to let go of areas of responsibility she didn't need to hold on to anymore. She also rewarded Susi with an increase in salary commensurate with her increased responsibilities. Susi is charged up again and on her way.

Kevin had a position as an education administrator. He loved his job and felt engaged and challenged by it. When he came to the work part of the empowerment journey, Kevin was sure it would just be a matter of fine-tuning a bit. Little did he know what was around the corner in his growth process!

Kevin was implementing very innovative projects within the guidance and counseling departments of his school district. His projects were highly effective and well regarded, but in his vision of the highest possibility for his work Kevin found himself changing the role of guidance counselors in public schools throughout his entire state.

He visualized boldly empowering guidance counselors throughout the public school system to teach their students the qualities of honesty, reliability, teamwork, and learning how to learn. Further in his vision he challenged counselors to learn to live what they hoped to teach and to set an example for healthy collaboration between students, teachers, and administrators. His vision included a new, positive curriculum to replace the old, negative one and ways to best implement this. Kevin was startled by the power of his vision. He felt as though he had no choice but to do everything he could to make this vision a reality.

We were thrilled to hear from Kevin several months following the workshop: "Those of us working with my project have a vision of guidance counselors being very much in a role which empowers students, teachers, and other counselors. We feel it is time to help counselors get out of their offices and away from the tons of paperwork that seem to have become their lot. Two weeks ago we went to our State Board of Education and requested that they budget $250,000 each year for the next five years to enable us to expand the project to include all schools in the state. They agreed, not only unanimously, but more importantly, enthusiastically. The thing that stirs them so is the concept of an empowerment curriculum. Although we call it a 'guidance curriculum,' we talk about it in empowerment terms."

Kevin decided to let his spirit soar during the ideal work vision and within three months had manifested something he had never dreamed about before he did the visioning exercise. Though he was fully content with his work, he dared to expand his vision and he's now living his dream.

Jack was a senior bank executive who had climbed up the corporate ladder and was now president of a regional bank that was doing quite well financially. He came into the Empowerment Workshop feeling uninspired about his work. He had no new challenges, and his deeper values just had no place for expression within his present work environment. He was starting to think about early retirement until he did the work vision exercise.

He came out of the work section of the workshop with bolts of energy. He envisioned his bank as a culture that empowered its employees; where they were encouraged to grow and realize more of their human potential; where they felt safe fully expressing their concerns; where love, caring, and kindness were acceptable and encouraged in the work environment; where people were motivated to release their creativity; where there was greater productivity and personal fulfillment as a result. He created the affirmation, "I create an empowered work culture in my bank." In his visualization he saw the people for whom he was responsible as happy, fulfilled, and productive.

One and a half years later he had created a wellness task force whose job it was to create an organizational culture that supported people in growing. He invited us to do an organizational empowerment training to launch this new program. Jack renewed his vision and aimed as high as possible. He knows that transforming a conservative organization culture is a slow process and he's thriving on the challenge.

EXERCISE

Work Affirmation and Visualization

Hearing how other people went for their dreams and manifested them may inspire you to go for yours. Go back and review the ideal work vision exercise and the issues you found that make up your growing edge. Synthesize what you have learned. Then, in your journal or the space below, write down your own affirmation and visualization that address your growing edge for work.

11

Spirituality

What allows you to feel your life has purpose and meaning? How do you nurture the internal dimension of yourself? Do you have a personal connection with the deeper rhythms of your life and of the Earth? How do you relate to the mystery of life? What offers you inspiration and hope? What allows you to feel deep joy? Do you feel connected to a higher power and intelligence? These questions require us to go deep within ourselves for the answers. Those answers shape and frame our spirituality.

Spirituality is a highly personal and intimate experience of our deeper nature. It should not be confused with the dogma and doctrine of religion. Discovering what allows the deeper parts of yourself to be fulfilled has nothing to do with other people's ideas about God. It has nothing to do with theological prescriptions of "do's" and "don'ts." Your relationship to your deeper nature determines your spiritual path. Your path is unlike anyone else's path. It is uniquely personal and evolves out of finding, uncovering, and nurturing *your* inner truth.

In response to the question "What does it mean to be spiritual?" people give many answers:

- To meditate, to love myself and others, and to begin to fulfill what is truly me.
- Claiming my creatorship and being truth and light.
- To be trusting and accepting that my inner process is unfolding exactly the way it should.
- Listening and living the guidance of my inner voice.
- To be the truth and keep my word.
- Acknowledging my physical existence as only a part of the universal order; seeking out the intentions of the cosmic coordinator.

The purpose of this chapter is to help you create or further your personal spiritual path. We will lead you through three explorations that will assist you in this process. The first will be an inner journey to your higher purpose.

Journey to Your Higher Purpose

Each of us comes to this planet to learn certain things and to accomplish certain things. Our higher purpose is the deeper reason for our being here. Understanding our higher purpose allows us to have available to our conscious minds those lessons that our evolving soul chose to learn in this life. When we create our lives in alignment with our higher purpose we have an extraordinary asset available to motivate us. Gandhi called it *satyagraha*, or soul force. It is the force of our deeper nature urging us to do whatever is necessary to learn our lessons and grow as a spiritual being. Some examples of a higher purpose might include:

- To raise a family and learn how to love.
- To learn that you are not a victim of circumstances but rather the creator of your own fate.
- To learn the lessons of manifesting a particular gift or talent.
- To trust that there is a benevolent and supporting higher intelligence—call it God or whatever word works for you—that cares about your well-being and with whom you can have a personal relationship.
- To learn the lessons of caring for people in need of help.
- To learn how to unconditionally love yourself.
- To learn to create financial abundance.
- To help the Earth and our human family through this challenging time in our evolution.
- To learn how to cooperate with others.
- To learn how to play and be joyful.

No one higher purpose is better than any other. To grow spiritually we each need to move toward fulfilling our unique higher purpose. The purpose of this next exercise is to help you understand your higher purpose or, if you understand it already, to take it to the next level.

As you ask about your higher purpose your inner self will communicate to you in an appropriate way. If you don't understand the communication, ask for clarity. One man who did this exercise was sure that he wasn't spiritual and that the following exercise had confirmed his belief. Frank felt he had "failed" spirituality because he had no meaningful higher purpose.

What had come to Frank during the exercise made no sense to him at all. His answer was "a shoe attached to a helicopter!" We suggested to him that he ponder those symbols.

On reflection he broke into a fit of laughter. His inner self was telling him that his higher purpose was for his soul (sole) to lift off (helicopter). Given Frank's offbeat, somewhat irreverent sense of humor, it was the perfect way for him to get the message. Frank has subsequently developed an active relationship with a new friend he calls the "Ultimate Big One." He writes poetry to his new friend all the time.

Keep yourself open on your inner journey to symbols, subtle feelings, any activity that unfolds in the visualization, and of course any obvious message you receive. Allow the process to flow easily and naturally in whatever way it does. Our inner guidance is totally available to us—all we need to do is ask.

EXERCISE

Your Higher Purpose

Allow approximately fifteen minutes to do this exercise. You will not need your journal during the exercise, but you will want to have it handy immediately afterward. Space has been left in case you do not have your journal. Find a quiet place where you will be undisturbed. Sit in a comfortable chair and put on some soft, relaxing music. The exercise is divided into several parts. Read a paragraph, then close your eyes and visualize. When you've completed that part, with soft eyes go on to the next paragraph. Get ready for a journey to your higher purpose.

1. Take several deep breaths and allow yourself to relax. Take a few moments to get still and find a quiet center within. In that quiet center begin to get in touch with the yearning that we all have to understand why we are here, the yearning to understand our higher purpose for being on the Earth. Prepare yourself for a journey in which you will seek spiritual counsel on a very important question: "What is my higher purpose and how may I manifest it more fully in my life?"

2. Imagine yourself on the outskirts of a very ancient forest. See yourself beginning to walk through this ancient forest. You walk farther and farther through this forest. As you walk you ponder the question you carry: "What is my higher purpose, and how may I manifest it more fully in my life?"

3. Soon you reach an opening in the forest and before you is a crystalline, clear pond. As you look into the pond you see an image. You ask this image the question you have been carrying with you: "What is my higher purpose and how may I manifest it more fully in my life?" Spend as much time as you need contemplating whatever you receive. If the answer is not clear, ask for more clarity.

4. It's now time to leave the pond and enter back into the ancient forest. As you walk back through the forest you continue to reflect on what you have learned. You walk farther and farther out of the forest. You walk back over the same trail and finally you're out of the forest. When you are ready gently open your eyes and bring yourself back to the here and now.

5. Maintaining soft eyes, write down or draw what you have received as an answer to your question. Describe or draw the particular image you saw in the pond and anything else of note about the journey. If the answer didn't come in words but in some other way, write down or draw what you experienced.

One man, an artist by profession, had the following experience: "The night before this exercise I had dreamed of a blond woman with whom I felt a deep intimacy. She had many other woman friends. Later, I also dreamed of touching my mother gently on the cheek.

"I begin the journey into the woods very skeptically. On my way I noticed a peculiar smell in the room, that of a woman's clean-washed, soapy hair, a wonderful freshness. Momentarily ignoring the visualization of being in the woods, I open my eyes and look around to see whose odor I had caught. I am sitting beside a sweaty man and other unlikely candidates; I conclude that I am imagining things, though the odor was so strong.

"Back on the trail I approach the pool expecting absolutely nothing to happen. Suddenly, out of the pool somebody hands me a birthday cake. I am stunned. This is the craziest thing that I ever expected. What the hell am I supposed to do with the cake? I dutifully begin to carry it out of the woods and finally come to rest on a hill. I think, 'This must be my birthday!' But why? I am perplexed, but feel light, happy, and grin-foolish.

"After the visualization was over I told my partner about my unusual experience. Her vision had been of a woman with long blond hair who had told her to love herself. Suddenly the smell of clean, close hair rushed back to me. Suddenly the blonde in my last night's dream came to life. Suddenly I felt my hand on my mother's cheek.

"I suddenly understood! My higher purpose is to celebrate my anima's birthday, the birth of my divine goddess! As a result of this higher purpose exercise I created the following affirmation, 'I celebrate the birth of my female divinity.' "

Another person reported: "As I looked in the pond I felt a puff of air against my cheek. I looked over and saw this big eagle sitting on my right shoulder. It was looking straight ahead. I realized that I was protected. The next thing I knew, I was flying. I'm soaring over the hills and I feel like a three-year-old. The eagle gave me the experience of trust in the universe. I realized my higher purpose was to develop trust in the universe and that this eagle would help me to do this."

We hope you now have a deeper understanding of your higher purpose and how you may manifest it more fully. If anything is still unclear to you, go back to your pond and ask for more clarity. If you had a particularly positive rapport with the entity or symbol you saw reflected in the pond, it can serve as a representation of your inner self. You can go to the pond and ask this being or symbol for guidance on other matters that are important to you. The more you cultivate and draw upon your inner self, the more adept you will become at receiving inner guidance and connecting with the deeper rhythm of your life.

The Profound in Your Daily Life

A central element in creating a spiritual path is a connection with something that allows us to transcend the everyday, mundane aspects of our lives. This connection allows us to gain perspective and distance from our human drama and allows us to feel a sense of the profound in our life. We need to have a personal sense of oneness with the whole pattern of life that animates the cosmos. We need to regularly experience wonder. An intellectual concept of God is dry and sterile compared to a personal relationship with something transcendent. We can't just read about it or listen to others talk about it. We need to directly experience it.

We can connect with this sense of wonder, oneness, awe, and profundity in many ways. Some experiences that might have transported you to a higher level of consciousness are:

- Being present at a birth.
- Witnessing death.
- A moment of intense beauty.
- A movie or book that poignantly depicts the human condition.
- A lucid dream.
- Euphoria after making love.
- Falling in love.
- An extraordinary piece of music.
- A moment when you were able to laugh at the whole human drama.

- Euphoria that results from physical exercise.
- A profound moment of experiencing nature.

These moments are available to any of us without us having to do anything other than be open and sensitive to them. They are experiences that allow us to transcend our everyday reality and recognize that we are part of something much larger than we can explain or understand. The ancients called this *The Mystery*. Each of these profound moments is a spiritual experience that you can use as a point of focus for a regular meditation practice. As you meditate on this moment your consciousness once again reexperiences a state of transcendence.

EXERCISE

Transcendence Meditation

Allow approximately ten minutes to do this exercise. You will need your journal. Space has been left in case your journal is not handy. Find a quiet place where you will be undisturbed. Sit in a comfortable chair and put on some soft, relaxing music and get set.

1. Scan your life and write down those experiences in which you transcended your normal everyday state of mind and connected with the profound in life. Look through the list above for inspiration, but don't be limited by this list. If you had any meditation or prayer experiences that were profound, you can also draw on these.

2. Choose the experience that was most profound for you. Take a few deep breaths and experience yourself back in that moment. Immerse yourself in that experience. Experience it as fully and thoroughly as if it were happening right now. Spend at least five minutes being fully present in this experience and allow it to take you where it will. When you feel ready, bring yourself back to your normal state of consciousness.

3. Notice how you're feeling right now. Notice how you're relating to life right now. Notice how regenerated you feel. Use this meditation to spiritually refresh yourself whenever you feel the need. It's an asset you have accumulated in your spiritual bank account.

Discovering Your Spiritual Gifts

We each come into life with certain spiritual gifts to assist us in our growth. Like our higher purpose, knowledge of our spiritual gifts is readily available if we ask for it. These gifts are the spiritual bounty with which we come to further our evolution and bless the planet. The native American tradition says that when you truly know your spiritual gifts, you are in a position to fulfill your higher purpose.

The next exercise is an opportunity to discover, or deepen your already existing knowledge of, your gifts. It is a very special and magical inner journey.

EXERCISE

Spiritual-Gifts Guided Visualization

Allow thirty to forty minutes to do this exercise. You will need your journal and colored pens or drawing materials. Space has been left in case you don't have your journal handy. Find a quiet place where you will be undisturbed. Sit in a comfortable chair and put on some soft, relaxing music. The guided visualization is divided into several parts. After each paragraph, close your eyes so you can more easily visualize. At certain points in the journey you will be guided to draw or record in your journal. Maintain soft eyes as you move in and out of the meditative state. Get yourself ready for a magical journey.

1. Take several deep breaths and feel yourself getting relaxed. In this journey you will be carrying a question that you will ask of those you meet. The question is "Please tell me one of my spiritual gifts that I have been given to help me on my path." We invite you to take this journey as your child self. Be open to wonder and magic. Take a few moments now to be in touch with your childlike spirit of wonder.

2. See yourself at the outskirts of the same forest you just visited for your higher-purpose journey. As you know by now, this forest is quite magical and has many surprises in it. Again begin to walk through this ancient forest. As you walk farther into the forest you come upon a large tree trunk with a door. Open the door and notice that there is a spiral ladder leading down into the tree trunk. You begin to climb down the spiral ladder until you are well below the surface of the Earth. You spiral down, down, down.

3. Finally you reach the end of the spiral ladder and come to another door. You open this door and enter a world of splendor and enlightenment. For several moments you just take in this extraordinary sight, listening to the wondrous sounds and delighting in what you see. As you are marveling you become aware of your ability to communicate with everything in your environment. You also discover your ability to fly!

4. As you begin to explore this world of splendor and enlightenment you find yourself attracted to a crystal. You develop a very special friendship with this crystal and ask your crystal friend this question: "Please tell me one of my spiritual gifts that I have been given to help me on my path." When you have received your answer, with soft eyes record or draw what you have received in your journal.

5. Thank your friend the crystal and say good-bye. As you continue to explore this world of splendor and enlightenment you hear a flower calling your name. Again, you develop a very special friendship with this flower. After a while you ask your flower friend this question: "Please tell me one of my spiritual gifts that I have been given to help me on my path." When you have received your answer, with soft eyes record or draw what you've received in your journal.

6. Thank your friend the flower and say good-bye. As you continue your adventure you come upon a great kingdom of animals. You begin to play with the animals. Gradually you are attracted to a certain animal with which you develop a special friendship. You ask your animal friend, "Please tell me one of my spiritual gifts that I have been given to help me on my path." When you have received your answer, with soft eyes record or draw what you have received in your journal.

7. As before, thank your animal friend and say good-bye. As you're leaving, a butterfly alights upon your shoulder and guides you as you fly together to the top of a mountain. Waiting for you on the mountaintop is a wise and loving person. Again, you develop a very special friendship with this person. You ask this wise and loving friend the question, "Please tell me one of my spiritual gifts I have been given to help me on my path." When you have received your answer, with soft eyes record or draw what you received in your journal.

8. Thank your friend and say good-bye. As you leave your friend on the mountaintop, you take to flight, fully enjoying the joy of flying. During your flight you fly through a giant rainbow. As you come out the other side of the rainbow you find yourself in the realm of spirit. Greeting you there is a spirit guide. You develop a special friendship with this spirit guide. When you feel ready, you ask your spirit guide friend your question: "Please tell me one of my spiritual gifts that I have been given to help me on my path." When you have received an answer, gently, with soft eyes, record or draw what you received in your journal.

9. Thank your spirit guide and say good-bye. Your spirit guide lets you know it's time to return to your regular world. You begin to fly back over this magical world of splendor and enlightenment, reflecting upon the gifts you have received. You fly back over your friend on the mountaintop, over your animal friend, your friend the flower, and finally over your crystal friend.

10. You arrive back at the door that opens to the spiral ladder. You take one more look, savoring this magical world, and then open the door leading up into the tree trunk. You begin climbing back up the spiral ladder, up and up the spiral ladder, until you reach the door that leads out of the tree trunk. Open the door and reenter the ancient forest. You begin to retrace your footsteps back through the forest. You come farther and farther out of the forest, until you are on the edge of the forest where you entered. When you are ready you leave the forest and come back to the here and now.

Spend a little time being with what you have just experienced. There is no rush to move on. Allow the magic of the journey to be with you. When you're ready you can read further.

The kinds of spiritual gifts people uncover are varied. Sometimes they are intangible gifts such as wisdom, love, compassion, kindness, integrity, generosity, gentleness, balance, trust, will, sensitivity, leadership, and intelligence. Sometimes they are very tangible gifts such as organizational know-how, athletic prowess, a Midas touch, healing powers, artistic ability, physical beauty, manual dexterity, and so on. Like every other part of life, there is no gift that is better than another. The special gifts that we each have are there to help us learn what we came here to learn. Our primary responsibility is to use the gifts that we have to the fullest of our ability.

The beings who tell us our gifts are themselves sometimes quite meaningful to many people who do this exercise. If this was so for you, you might find it exciting to reconnect with one or more of them at a future time. They can be special spiritual friends who help you on your life's journey. If you feel the need for spiritual counsel above and beyond that which your own inner self can provide, ask your spiritual friends for advice.

Walking Your Spiritual Path

With knowledge of your higher purpose, your special way to connect with the mystery, and your inner gifts, you have all the elements you need to make up your unique spiritual path. Only *you* can determine how to walk this path. How slowly or fast you walk is completely your choice. *You are totally in charge and responsible for your own spiritual evolution.* You can certainly get inspiration from a spiritual group, religion, or teacher, but ultimately the spiritual journey is a solo journey. An interior life that is constantly unfolding and deepening will motivate and excite you to keep walking your spiritual path. Like every other part of life, your inner life needs nourishment and cultivation to remain alive and growing. Let's look at some ways to do this.

- **Develop an Ongoing Relationship with Your Inner Self** To be in touch with the deeper rhythms of your life you need to take time each day to relate to your inner self in silence. If the words "inner self" don't speak to you, choose words that do. There are many to choose from: higher self, God-self, soul, inner friend, Father within, Mother within, Spirit within. You can make up your own, like Frank's "Ultimate Big One." Whatever you call it, you need to take time each day to cultivate this inner relationship to renew and refresh yourself spiritually. It is this daily interaction that gives you the energy and inspiration to create a life based on your own inner truth.

Meditation is the method most ideally suited for this, as its explicit purpose is to quiet your mind so that you can attune to your deeper nature. If you don't have a meditation practice and are interested in developing one, consult our bibliography. Along with deepening your access to your inner self, meditation has many other rewards. Vimala Thalzar, an Eastern meditation teacher, says this of meditation in her lecture "Why Meditate":

"Silence has not been explored in your culture. Meditation offers the silence and balance. In this state of silence there is no tension. The wholeness of silence begins to heal the body and the mind. A new quality of perception, a new quality of response is available to us through the silence. Through the silence we gain an intimate relationship with ourself, the whole and the timelessness of life."

Whether it be through a meditation practice or another means for getting silent, *a daily interaction with your inner self is an essential ingredient in walking your spiritual path.*

- **Align Your Actions with Your Higher Purpose** Knowing your higher purpose and the inner assets you have to help to achieve this purpose is a remarkable blessing. You may not know exactly how to get where you're going at every moment, but you know your purpose for being on the Earth. You have a direction. Most people just stumble along through life never quite sure why they're doing what they're doing. They adopt the dominant beliefs of the culture, their parents, and their religion. They never develop their own inner truth and consequently never feel very satisfied.

To stay on your path you need to continually be aligning your actions with your higher purpose, asking, "Is what I'm doing aligned with my higher purpose?" "Does this activity further my higher purpose?" It's important to remember that your higher purpose has nothing to do with moral prescriptions, with do's and don't's. It has nothing to do with being religious, yet it can include deep religious observance. Your higher purpose revolves around the lessons your soul wants to learn in this life. When you are acting in alignment with your higher purpose, you will feel inwardly satisfied.

• **Develop a Spiritual Support System** Walking your path is easier around others who are also on a spiritual path. It inspires and encourages you to deepen your own spiritual practice. This is the primary reason churches, temples, spiritual brotherhoods and sisterhoods came into existence. A spiritual support group is primarily oriented toward interior life. Sometimes this can be combined with a personal growth support system—it's important to recognize the distinction.

A personal growth support system is often focused on issues that are externally or psychologically oriented. This complements a spiritual support system but is not the same. The purpose of a spiritual support system is to meditate together, pray together, chant together, celebrate the joy of being spiritually awake together through singing and dancing, share insights and spiritual experiences back and forth with others, and get support and feedback when we feel spiritually stuck.

You may be part of an existing group that, with a little tinkering, will provide you with the kind of spiritual nourishment you need. You may have to create your own group. If you do the latter, it gives you the opportunity to create the group exactly the way you want it. To maintain intimacy and quality communication the ideal group size is four to eight people. Sometimes people set up a small group within the framework of a larger group or class that meets regularly.

• **Spend Time with Nature** Another form of spiritual support is being with nature. Activities like taking quiet walks by the water or through the woods, sitting in a garden, and sailing can be very spiritually renewing. For some this is the primary way of connecting with the deeper rhythm of life. For all of us it provides an opportunity to slow down and become tranquil. When we're in this state of mind we can listen more closely to our inner selves and feel more connected with our life-support system, the Earth.

• **Accept Other Spiritual Paths** As we come to more fully understand that Earth is a school, with each of us here to learn different spiritual lessons, our ability to accept others greatly increases. *Our spiritual lessons are not better or worse than anyone else's—they are different.* It is to learn these lessons that we create our spiritual path. As we integrate this fundamental truth into our world view, we feel secure in our own spiritual path and more accepting of other paths. We come to understand that each of us must create his or her own spiritual path. We move from wanting others to be like us, and negatively judging them when they are not, into accepting them. We move from accepting others into encouraging them to find their own paths.

• **Become a Conscious Co-creator** If you were the creator of the universe, how would you like to interact with human beings? Would you like to interact with human beings who couldn't make decisions without asking you for advice at every turn in the road, or would you like to interact with human beings who had developed inner knowledge and wisdom, had learned to trust their inner guidance, and periodically came to you as a friend seeking advice? The former is like a child asking father or mother what to do. The latter is like the mature adult who relates as one friend to another.

As we travel along our spiritual paths a maturation process starts taking place in which we move from a dependent relationship with something outside of ourselves to a trust in our own inner knowing. *We move from being an instrument of some higher power to a co-creator with this higher power.* We move from being a victim of circumstances on Earth to being a co-creator of its evolution.

Whether you like it or not, you are a creative force in the universe. You are constantly co-creating the world through what you believe and the actions you take. Taking responsibility to consciously direct your thoughts and actions toward the end of helping evolve a better world is just the next level of empowerment.

The creator of the universe has a role—creating the evolution game and supporting us when we need help. And we have a role—playing in the evolution game as a creator. When we play the game wholeheartedly our personal evolution and the evolution of the world take place. By expanding our framework for the events of our lives to include helping the Earth evolve we take our power to a new level. This stretch furthers our spiritual evolution. It's quite a game!

A wonderful story describing this co-creation process is told by Marc Gellman. It is entitled "Partners."

> *Before there was anything, there was God, a few angels, and a gigantic, spinning, swirling glob of rocks and water with no place to go.*
>
> *The Angels said to God, "Why don't you clean up this mess?"*
>
> *So God took all the rocks out of the swirling glob, put them in one place, and said, "I will call this place the universe. Some of the rocks will be planets, some will be stars, and some will be just rocks."*
>
> *Then God took all the water from the swirling glob and spread it around the universe, saying, "Some of this water will be oceans, some will be clouds, and some will be just water."*
>
> *Then the angels asked God, "Is the world finished?"*
>
> *God answered, "NOPE!"*
>
> *On some of the rocks God placed growing things—and creeping things—and things which only God knows what they are! And when God had done all this, the angels looked around the universe and said, "Well, it's neater but is it finished?"*
>
> *God answered, "NOPE!"*
>
> *God made a man and a woman from some of the water and dust and said, "Look, I'll give you the whole world, but you have to finish it."*
>
> *"Now you look!" they said. "We can't finish the world without your help—so maybe—we could be partners."*
>
> *God warned them, "If we're going to be partners, sometimes you might get*

angry at me, and sometimes I might get angry at you, but even so, none of us can stop finishing the world—that's the deal." And they all agreed to the deal.

Then the angels asked God, "Is the world finished?"
God smiled and answered, "I don't know. Go ask my partners."

Co-creating the future of the Earth with God is the best game in town! No spiritual path should be without it.

Your Spiritual Growing Edge

To find out what your spiritual growing edge may be, think about your responses to the three exercises you just completed. Did you notice any limiting beliefs that arose to stop you?

To further assist you in finding your growing edge, below is a list of some common limiting beliefs and their turnarounds. Then we'll share some stories of how others have worked with their spirituality growing edges.

LIMITING BELIEF: I can't be spiritual and also be financially successful/sexual/powerful/desire worldly things.
TURNAROUND: Spiritual does not mean anti-material. I imbue my life with spiritual values such as joy, peace, harmony, love, beauty, kindness, generosity, and reverence, which adds quality to my material existence.

LIMITING BELIEF: To be spiritual I must follow a code of conduct laid out by a religion/guru/writer of a spiritual book.
TURNAROUND: My spirituality grows out of my own self-knowledge. I trust it and found my actions upon it.

LIMITING BELIEF: To grow spiritually I must remove myself from the snares of the world.
TURNAROUND: My life in the world is where I practice my spirituality.

LIMITING BELIEF: Spirituality is too removed from daily life to be practical and useful.
TURNAROUND: The more I am in alignment with what gives my life meaning and purpose, the more I release my passion into success in the world. My daily life is an expression of my inner passion.

LIMITING BELIEF: Spirituality means giving over control of my life to some higher power that's outside of me.
TURNAROUND: God's will is my own highest consciousness in this moment.

LIMITING BELIEF: To be spiritual I must subdue my ego.
TURNAROUND: My ego is the form that holds my personality. I allow my

personality to grow until it expands beyond the ego container and touches the infinite freedom of spirit.

LIMITING BELIEF: The nature of life on this planet is suffering.
TURNAROUND: Life on this planet is whatever I make it. My life is about love, play, joy, harmony, and oneness.

LIMITING BELIEF: The goal of spirituality is to get off the planet/go to heaven/attain nirvana/become God-realized, as soon as possible, and our actions should all be directed toward this end.
TURNAROUND: I learn the lessons of Earth on Earth and nowhere else.

LIMITING BELIEF: A sign of spiritual evolution is the acquisition of special powers.
TURNAROUND: A sign of my spiritual evolution is wisdom, kindness, and love; special powers are a sideline.

LIMITING BELIEF: To evolve spiritually I need to master sacred esoteric texts, have a guru, and spend years meditating.
TURNAROUND: To evolve spiritually I need to learn what I came to Earth to learn. It may or may not include a guru, scriptures, and meditation.

LIMITING BELIEF: My life is a mess because of my bad karma.
TURNAROUND: I accept where I am at this moment and take responsibility to create my future. I am in charge of my destiny.

LIMITING BELIEF: The world is full of corrupt, evil people who are leading it down a road of destruction.
TURNAROUND: I take responsibility to create the world as a beautiful and sacred place filled with beings committed to their own and the planet's evolution.

LIMITING BELIEF: God is a male figure with a lot of power who will punish me if I don't do the right thing.
TURNAROUND: I create God as a loving, kind, playful, wise, powerful friend. We play together co-creating the universe.

When Michael did the Empowerment Workshop he was feeling disempowered spiritually. He had recently left a spiritual group that laid out a prescribed path that he had to follow in order to grow spiritually. There were lots of do's and don't's and dogmas. He had not been encouraged to develop his own relationship to God and his inner self; rather he was told the spiritual leader knew best and had all the answers. Michael didn't trust that he could find his own inner truth and be in charge of his own spiritual development.

When he did the higher-purpose exercise he broke into tears. For the first time in his life he felt he could go within himself and get answers to important questions. Michael discovered that his higher purpose was to learn to trust the God within and not to rely on outside sources to tell him how to act and think. This insight was reinforced in the meditation on the profound in daily life. In that meditation Michael felt a very close relationship with nature and realized that this was an important way for him to connect with God.

Michael's affirmation was "I trust my own inner knowing and path to God." His visualization was seeing himself at his favorite spot in nature, feeling totally connected with himself and all of creation.

When Joan came to the Empowerment Workshop she felt very inspired to work on all the parts of her life—except spirituality. She just didn't know what to make of this part of life nor did she really pay much attention to it. During the exercises in the spirituality part of the workshop she didn't expect a lot to happen.

During the higher-purpose exercise Joan learned that her purpose was to love herself, and through this she would experience the enormous love of the universe. Her growing-edge work in the other parts of life had been precisely about loving herself. She began to feel more excited and intrigued as we moved into the spiritual-gifts exercise. She received the following gifts to help her on her path: a compassionate heart, gentle patience, lighthearted humor, vulnerability, and a sense of adventure. She felt these were the most appropriate gifts in helping her love herself.

During the meditation on the profound in daily life she reconnected with a moment when she felt the benevolent love of a higher power in nature. This crystallized in her mind that there was a loving higher presence that cared for her.

By now she realized spirituality was not something separate from the rest of her life, but rather an integral part of life that supported and infused all the other parts. Joan realized that by nurturing the spiritual part of her life she was helping all her other growing edges. She created this affirmation and visualization: "I nurture my spirituality, and this sprinkles love on all the other areas of my life." Her visualization was taking quiet time to meditate.

Several months later she wrote, "I now understand my spiritual life is the foundation that informs all other areas of life. I continue to be committed to my affirmations and meditation. My spiritual life is growing and sending ripples out through the rest of my life. I am living with more joy and more fullness than I thought possible."

When Brad came to the Empowerment Workshop his greatest longing was to feel a personal sense of spirituality. He had only experienced spirituality intellectually through books and others' words. His growing edge was clearly to create a personal relationship with something larger than himself.

During the meditation on connecting with the profound in everyday life, Brad went back to his grandmother's death. He reexperienced the mystery of that moment, the feelings of awe, profound love, and the precious fragility of life. He remembered feeling the miraculous largeness of the universe as it enfolded him and his grandmother in both life and death. As he came out of the meditation Brad felt charged. He felt that he had received what he had wanted—a personal way to connect with the mystery of life. He created this affirmation and visualization: "I take time each day to touch the mystery of life." His visualization was seeing himself connected to the fragile life on this planet, yet also part of something much larger.

Margaret was a therapist who had been on a spiritual path for many years when we met her at the Empowerment Workshop. Though she was very happy with her spirituality, she was seeking her next stretch in this area. Her growing edge was to find that next stretch and go for it!

During the higher-purpose exercise Margaret learned that her purpose was to be more than a psychological guide for people—she was to be a spiritual guide. Accepting that she was a spiritual guide was definitely a stretch. She was still considering this new edge as she went into the spiritual-gifts journey. She received the following gifts: unconditional love, light, service to humanity, a still clear mind, and spiritual vision. Margaret was overwhelmed by the beauty and depth of her gifts.

Margaret became aware that her spiritual growing edge was to fully own her gifts and accept that she was a spiritual guide. She recognized that the primary focus of her life and work with people was spiritual, yet she still viewed herself in a more traditional role as a therapist. The shift she needed to make was subtle, yet dramatic. She crafted this affirmation and visualization: "I joyfully own my purpose as a spiritual guide and dedicate my life to spirit." In her visualization she stood with her hands outstretched toward the light.

EXERCISE

Spirituality Affirmation and Visualization

It's time to create your own affirmation and visualization that address your growing edge for spirituality. Review the higher-purpose exercise, the transcendence meditation, and the spiritual gifts you have discovered. Look through the limiting beliefs and turnarounds for more insight on your growing edge. Create an affirmation and visualization that address your growing edge for spirituality. We wish you joy as you walk your path.

Part Three

Returning Home

12

Always Growing! Making Your Passion Happen

C ongratulations! You have just completed a remarkable inner journey! You are returning home with new learnings, insight, self-knowledge, and growth. You've journeyed deep into yourself to get to this point and should feel proud of your accomplishment.

In the course of this inner adventure you have thoroughly explored your life, discovered what it is that you deeply believe, made changes in outdated beliefs, and crafted new visions of how you want your life to look. In all likelihood some of these visions have already started to manifest; many more will in the near future. Your growing edges are enlivened and bursting with vitality and potential.

It's now time to integrate this highly charged potential into your daily life so that it can come to fruition. To do this you need to set up a structure for working with your affirmations and visualizations on a daily basis and build a support system to strengthen the growth you have undertaken. Let's start by looking at how to work with your affirmations and visualizations over time.

Guidelines for Applying Your Affirmations and Visualizations

• **Nourish Them Daily** You have created potent mental seeds that need nourishment in order to grow. *The way you nourish your affirmations and visualizations is through your belief in your vision manifesting.* The amount of time required need not be more than five minutes a day. The key is not quantity of time, but quality of time. You need to be very present when you are saying your affirmations and visualizing. Be attentive to any mental weeds or limiting beliefs that have cropped up in your mental garden. If you notice a limiting belief, use one of the mental clearing tools to remove it. If you find that it is too deeply rooted, back up one step on your growing edge.

The purpose of this time devoted to your affirmations and visualizations is to come to deeply believe that your vision will manifest. It is this deep belief that allows the mental seed to germinate and come to fruition. The time you set aside each day creates and energizes this state of knowing.

• **Find a Niche** To make sure your mental seeds get nourished daily you need to set up a specific time and place to work with them. You are establishing a new habit in your life. To make sure it becomes established you have to apply your will and plan for it. If you remember that the reason you are taking these five minutes for yourself is to bring the things that are most important to you into your life, you won't have any problem staying motivated. It takes about a month of doing your affirmations and visualizations every day to establish a pattern.

A good time to do your affirmations and visualizations is when you first wake up. You are fresh, and you can energize your day with them. Another good time is just before you go to bed. This allows you to take them into the dream state with you. Another time people find appropriate is while exercising. The state of mental alertness and physical vitality generates high-quality mental energy for them.

You need to choose a time that works best for you and then be consistent. Commit to one time of day for thirty days and see how it feels. Experiment until you find the right niche. Write down here or in your journal the time you have chosen:

• **Create a Personal Form** There are many different ways that you can work with your affirmations and visualizations. The key is to find a form that motivates you.

The most common form is to read your affirmation silently from your journal and then visualize your image. Allow it to sink in and impregnate your consciousness. It helps to have your mind reasonably quiet. Taking a few deep breaths will help do this. If you have a meditation practice, do your affirmation and visualization work after you have meditated and are quiet. Stay with the affirmation and visualization until you feel they have sunk in. Sometimes this takes a few seconds, sometimes a minute or more.

Other forms that you might enjoy include:

- Writing out each affirmation one or more times and repeating it as you are writing.
- Recording it on an audio tape with music in the background and a space for you to repeat it.
- Having an inspiring piece of music in the background as you are affirming and visualizing.
- Singing your affirmation.
- Having an artist draw your visualizations.
- Putting your affirmations in strategic locations such as the refrigerator, checkbook, office, running shoes.
- Saying self-esteem affirmations in front of a mirror.
- Physically enacting your affirmation or visualization through a special movement or dance.
- Creating your visualization in clay or some other form of sculpture.
- Painting or drawing your visualization each day.

There is no one form to use. It's completely up to your creativity and what works best for you. Do choose one form and commit to using it for at least two weeks. This is enough time to see if it's the right form for you. If it's not, choose another form. Experiment some more. Keep tinkering with the form until you find the one that appeals most to your temperament. You may discover that a variety of forms is appropriate. For now the key is to become familiar enough with a particular form to know if it's right for you. Write down here or in your journal your next action step you plan to take in creating a form:

• **How Many to Work with at One Time** As with the other guidelines, there is no hard-and-fast rule. *How many affirmations and visualizations you choose to work with is a function of the psychic intensity of your growth issues.* If you are going through major changes, you may want to work actively with only two or three and have the others simmering on the back burner. Most people like to at least be paying attention to all the vital parts of their lives, even if they are working dynamically with only their most crucial growing edges. You may also find that you have a very important growth issue that requires more than one affirmation.

Generally speaking, if you don't have any all-consuming growth issues, you should be able to work with seven or eight affirmations and visualizations without a strain.

• **Regular Upkeep** Because you are creating affirmations and visualizations that are addressing your growing edges, you will outgrow them. This is not only to be expected but desired. It's a statement that says you're growing and your affirmations are working.

How do we know when we have outgrown our present vision? The most obvious way is when we look around and notice that we have accomplished whatever it is we are affirming and visualizing. This is easily discerned if we are dealing with very obvious, physically demonstrable issues such as money, work, or our bodies. However, psychological, emotional, and spiritual changes we are attempting to bring about are more subtle.

In this domain boredom is an excellent way to discern that change has taken place! If saying your affirmation starts to feel like tedious drudgery, something has changed. To respond to this change you may need to adjust a word or phrase in your affirmation, change your visualization, or approach the growth issue from another angle. The essential thing is to be attentive to your internal response and make changes in the affirmation, visualization, or growth issue accordingly.

Sometimes when we have been working on an issue and have achieved what we desired, we continue to hold on simply because we have grown accustomed to having the issue in our life. To minimize this try setting time aside twice a year to do a major overhaul of your growing edges. We find spring and fall to be good times. Without looking at your present affirmations and visualizations, ask yourself, "What are my next growing edges?" They may come out being the same, but often you will find that you have grown beyond those edges and it's time to move on. If this is the case, celebrate the harvest and plant new seeds.

• **Attentiveness to Your Thoughts During the Day** A daily practice of working with your affirmations and visualizations energizes your visions on a regular basis. Along with this more formal time, *it's important to be aware of what you're thinking about throughout the day.* Are you thinking about your visions as if they're successful? Are you seeing images of your visions as fully manifested? When you talk to others about your visions do you describe them in positive terms? How you think and talk during the day is very significant. It either reinforces or negates the more formal work you are doing.

You don't need to burden yourself affirming or visualizing all day, but you do need to be attentive to your thoughts. If you find yourself with a limiting belief, simply notice it and kick in your affirmation. If a fear comes up, just notice it and turn it around. If you are thinking about your vision in the future tense, bring it into the present tense.

Moment by moment we create our reality. You are now endowed with self-awareness and have the ability to step out of a thought and change it. You have done the hard work of acquiring the self-awareness to *notice* what you are thinking. *Changing* the thought is the easy work. It is a reward for the in-depth self-exploration work you have done.

Designing a Personal Growth Support System

It's now time to design an ongoing structure to support you in taking all the personal growth work you have done and establishing it firmly in your life.

The daily stresses of life tend to wear us down if we don't have anything to buoy us up again. In spite of our best efforts to maintain our growth, that vital spark that keeps us on our growing edges often flickers. To keep our spark glowing we need regular inspiration and renewal. The purpose of a personal growth support system is to provide the ongoing inspiration and renewal to enable you to sustain your growth over time. It can include some or all of the following components:

• **Professional Support Team** These are people who support you in some clearly defined way. This team might include a therapist to help you work with emotional and psychological issues, a financial advisor to help you stay on track with your money, a professional mentor to help you advance in your career, a body worker to help deal with physical stress, and a spiritual counselor with whom you can share your spiritual life.

These relationships don't just happen. They require that you recognize their importance and build these people into your life. They are your quality-of-life support system.

1. Take some time now and decide who should make up your personal growth support team. Write down the categories of people, such as therapist, nutritionist, chiropractor, financial advisor, masseuse, career mentor, and so on. If you know particular people who can fill these roles, write their names next to each category. If you have done some of this work in other chapters, refer back to that part of your journal and place their names here.

2. Once you have listed the categories and the people, write down your next action step for each category. For example, let's say you want to do more in-depth work with one of the emotional issues that has come up. The action step might be "Next week, start asking friends if they know of any therapists whose work is empowering." Make your action steps as specific and concrete as possible.

• **Peer Support Group** A peer support group is dedicated to growth around a particular issue or to growth in general. Issue support groups might focus on relationships, a twelve-step program, professional development, spiritual development, prosperity consciousness, and so on. More general support groups are dedicated to any of the growth issues you are working on in your life. One of the more common forms is as a men's or women's support group.

After each Empowerment Workshop, support groups are formed by those participants who would like to use the empowerment method to keep their growing edges alive. If you know other people who have read this book, you might want to form such a group.

The form is very simple. People meet once a month for three or four hours and work on their growth issues of the past month. They create affirmations and visualizations that address their growing edges. At the end of the gathering each person shares the growth issue they worked on, reads his or her affirmation and visualization, and gets acknowledged and encouraged by the group. A spirit of celebration permeates these gatherings.

If you decide to create an empowerment support group, feel free to modify and build on this form. Co-create as a group to meet your needs.

What kind of peer support group or groups would you like to create for yourself? A couples group, men's group, women's group, empowerment support group? Research to see if there is an existing group you might join. More often than not you will have to start your own group. Your next action step might then be "Call up the people I know who I would like to be part of a personal growth support group and ask them if they're interested." Write down the next action step you will take to bring this about.

Putting It All Together

• ***Choose a Home for Your Affirmations and Visualizations*** At this point your affirmations and visualizations are scattered throughout this book or your journal. To facilitate working with them on a daily basis, go back through your journal or this book and put them all in one place. The last few pages of your journal may work well. If you don't have a journal handy, we have left space below.

When you have placed all these mental seeds in one location, take a few moments to review the work you have done. Celebrate your accomplishment. Acknowledge yourself for the commitment you have made to your growth and well-being. Acknowledge yourself for stepping off the treadmill of life, out of our cultural hypnosis. Acknowledge yourself for taking time to examine your life and for how you want to create it. Recognize this moment for the significance of what it represents—you, as an empowered person, forging your own destiny! In the space below gather all the mental seeds (leave the Personal Power space blank for now).

Affirmations and Visualizations	Personal Power
1.	
2.	
3.	
4.	
5.	
6.	
7.	
etc.	

● **Use Your Personal Power to Sustain Your Growth** It's time to draw on the sources of personal power that you cultivated in Chapter Three—those that provide you with the ability to sustain your growth over time. The seven sources of personal power are:

- Commitment
- Discipline
- Support system
- Inner guidance
- Lightness
- Love
- Finding your own truth

Go back over the affirmations and visualizations you have just listed. Next to each one write down which sources of personal power will help you to manifest it. For example, you might decide that for your body vision to manifest, you need discipline and commitment; for your relationship vision you need love; for work, finding your own truth; and for money you need lightness. When you have done this you will have a sense of what sources of personal power you need to cultivate further.

You very well may discover that a pattern emerges, that the same sources of personal power are needed for all or most of your affirmations. This is a very important indicator. It tells you how important it is to bring that source of personal power into your life.

In addition to self-awareness and metaphysical knowledge, to create a more abundant and fulfilling life you need personal power. You create personal power in the same way you create anything else—by focusing your mental attention on it. Take time each day to cultivate the particular sources of personal power you need to sustain your growth for the long journey—your whole life.

Now go back to the rooms in your guided visualization at the end of Chapter Three and spruce up or redesign those that represent the sources of power you want to cultivate. If a particular room needs to be redesigned, take the time now to make the room exactly as you want it. Make the room as much fun and enjoyable as possible. Then write out or draw this visualization next to the space that contains your affirmations and visualizations. Each day start your affirmation and visualization work by visiting the power rooms you are cultivating. This will establish the right atmosphere in which you can manifest your visions.

● **An *Invitation* to *Participate* in the *Empowerment* Workshop** We have mentioned our Empowerment Workshop many times throughout this book. It has been our teacher and a teacher to many throughout the world. If you feel inspired to have this direct experience, please join us. It's a rich opportunity to further the work you've just done in the company of others who are also committed to their growth and full potential. We welcome you! Information on how to participate is listed in the "Further Support" section at the back of the book.

You have journeyed long and learned much. As you apply what you've learned over the next few months and years, be patient. The journey is the destination. We experience the momentary satisfaction in manifesting what we have envisioned and celebrate the wonder of it. And then we ask ourselves, "What's next?" and we're on the road again. The journey is endless, so be gentle with yourself and with life.

Epilogue

In closing we want to share with you something very special from our lives. It's the story of how our personal empowerment came to include creating and manifesting a very large vision, a vision of hope and possibility for our world, a vision of our power and capacity to create the world that we want.

From September 16 through December 11, 1986, twenty-five million people and forty-five heads of state in sixty-two countries participated in passing a torch of peace around the world, encircling it with light. The torch in turn shed light on what was working in the world—local self-help projects that were creating solutions to community challenges. This event was called the First Earth Run; it was a celebration of our possibility to live in harmony with each other and our Earth. We organized it under the banner of the United Nations International Year of Peace; our global partner and sponsor was the United Nations Children's Fund (UNICEF).

Twenty thousand people gathered to participate in the ceremony on the grounds of the U.N. on September 16, 1986, to launch the flame on its journey around the world.

More than 500 million people were made aware of the event through the media. In the United States, ABC's *Good Morning America* provided unprecedented television coverage; tracking the event every week for the twelve weeks of its global journey.

This all grew out of a vision and the knowledge that we can create any vision we believe in—the essence of personal empowerment. As we kept experiencing the empowerment process in our own life, and seeing others experience its power in their lives, it was only a matter of time before we were ready to own a larger vision, a vision of making a difference in the world—the whole world. It was quite an adventure! We'll share some of this adventure—and what we learned along the way—with you from our different points of view.

For me, David, the creation and manifestion of the First Earth Run was a ten-year process. In 1976 I organized the U.S. Bicentennial Torch Relay as a way to rekindle the human and spiritual values upon which America was founded. It went through all fifty states and was wonderfully received. Tens of thousands of Americans were inspired by this event, and President Ford honored the initiative as one of the major contributions to the Bicentennial celebration.

As the flame was being extinguished on August 16 after its journey through America, I had a strong impulse to see this fire continue around the world. That was the birth of the vision—passing the fire from person to person around the world to celebrate our potential to live in harmony with each other and the Earth. It was a positive vision of hope and possibility designed to replace the many negative visions that permeate the psyche of the people of our Earth.

I attempted to create this event in 1979 as part of the U.N. International Year of the Child, but I did not have very much success. I couldn't raise the money or convince people that it could be done. I was not skilled enough, and the timing didn't seem to be right for a global event. By the end of this attempt I had spent my savings and was feeling quite frustrated and disappointed.

Then, out of the blue, the 1980 Olympic Torch Relay fell into my lap. I was invited to organize the Winter Olympic Torch Relay that went from Olympia, Greece, to Lake Placid, New York.

My favorite part of this experience was picking up the flame in Greece. I flew on Air Force One to Athens. There we took another plane and then a bus to the little town of Olympia. Just as I arrived I saw the flame being processed in the ancient ritual form by twelve Greek priestesses. They moved with such an appreciation and love for the light they were carrying that I was inspired. They treated it with great respect for its symbolic value to the world, as one of the few sacred symbols that still has integrity on this planet. As I witnessed this I was moved to tears. When the flame entered Air Force One, one of the flight attendants said that this was the most special passenger she had ever flown.

Instead of taking the fire around the world, a billion people watched the fire come into Lake Placid to start the Winter Games. My vision was partially manifested, and for several years I felt complete. I hung up my torch and once again started doing human potential trainings. About six months later I met Gail, we fell in love, and decided to create the Empowerment Workshop.

As we did the Empowerment Workshop each month, what we experienced was a deep integration into our beings of the ideas we were teaching. Although we had both worked with the manifestation process successfully before we began the workshop, we were now learning this process at a cellular level. After three years of this we knew it was time to expand. The mental seed that I had planted seven years earlier, and which had lain dormant for four years, was once again germinated. Maybe this time—definitely this time—it would work.

I felt that with Gail's help we had enough personal power to take the light around the world. If we were successful the world would be a better, more hopeful place as a result of our effort. I told her that our lives—and the financial comfort we had achieved—would be totally disrupted. Gail said, "Is there a choice? If we can make a difference, we need to go for it." And so we did!

For the next three years we developed the First Earth Run as full-time volunteers, offering the Empowerment Workshop on weekends. I learned what it meant to persevere, to continually refine your vision when you get feedback that it's not working. I learned about all the qualities of personal power and how important they are to creating a vision. I learned anew that when you are creating your own truth, commitment and discipline help move you forward, and inner guidance, love, and lightness help you keep perspective.

I learned how important trust in the universe is when you know the final destination but you don't have a clue as to how you'll get there. I learned how important believing in myself and my vision was if I was to get others—from a volunteer to a head of state—to join in. I learned how important a positive attitude and flowing with change were, as up to one month before the event we had not firmly secured our financing.

In effect I spent three years intensively learning all the lessons in this book and then testing them out in the field of play. They allowed me to be effective and the event to manifest—ten years later—almost exactly as I had envisioned it in August 1976. On that day my vision was seeing the flame in the General Assembly Hall of the United Nations being passed to the Secretary General by a child, who reminded us why we need to change the future now. I then saw the Secretary General, moved to tears and deeply inspired, passing it from leader to leader within the General Assembly Hall. And that's the way it happened, not all at once, but over eighty-six days.

U.N. Secretary General Javier Perez de Cuellar was moved to tears as he received the flame from a child and launched it on its journey around the world. It passed through the hands of millions of people and most of the world's major leaders and eventually was handed back to the Secretary General in the General Assembly Hall as the guest of honor in a special session called to celebrate its return. My greatest dream had manifested with all the elements I had envisioned—and much more.

Now I have more than hope; I know for certain that we, the people living on this planet, have the ability to create the world the way we all, in our hearts, want it to be. At this very moment we have the ability to create a peaceful planet, dedicated to caring for all its inhabitants and our fragile life-support system. We have the ability to create a planet full of kindness, caring, love, and generosity, a planet where people are developing their full human potential, a planet where we use our creativity to make it a better and healthier place to live, for us and for the children who inherit it when we leave.

U.N. Secretary General Perez de Cuellar holding the torch at launch on September 16, 1986. At his right is Jim Grant, the executive director of UNICEF, global sponsor for the First Earth Run.

This is the vision that the rest of my life is dedicated to manifesting. The more who help, adding their variations on the theme, the sooner we can create it.

For me, Gail, the seeds of my future involvement in the First Earth Run were born when I was very young. My love affair with the natural world is one of the strongest memories of my childhood. I vividly recall endless days spent exploring brooks and fields and climbing every tree within my childhood territory. I remember my mother peeling off my wet, muddy clothes and examining the treasures I had brought home from my quests—rocks, sticks, and wildflowers. I was, quite literally, in love with this Earth, and this love of the Earth inspired and sustained me during the most exciting and challenging experience of my life—the First Earth Run.

Another experience that prepared me for the Earth Run was the time spent living and working in other cultures. I saw the bigger picture, recognized how fortunate I was, and wanted to make a contribution toward creating a better world.

Another major influence came at home in the United States. I was deeply involved in both the antiwar activism of the sixties and the women's movement of the seventies. In both these grass-roots experiences I learned something very important: I make a difference.

The final influence on me was the Empowerment Workshop. Here I had the privilege of being with many people committed to both their own well-being and the planet's. Their commitment gave me an enormous sense of hope that we had the power to make it as a human family.

On New Year's Day 1983, David and I went to see the film *Gandhi*. It had just been released, and we stood in a long line in Manhattan for hours in order to get tickets. Nearly half the audience was Indian and all around me Hindi was being spoken. Though I had read Gandhi's writings and long considered him a mentor, I was not prepared for the power of the experience that was about to unfold.

I cried through the entire film. I felt as if all the major threads of my personal empowerment were being woven together in front of my eyes: my love of the Earth, my yearning to make a contribution toward a better world, my understanding that I could make a difference, and my feeling of hope. The inspiration of Gandhi's life, exquisitely portrayed through Attenborough's film, integrated the separate strands of my process into a whole. It took me several weeks after the film to understand this, but what I did immediately know was that something inside me had shifted. I felt moved and empowered. I wanted to act.

I created an affirmation to attract a vehicle for expressing this newfound inspiration and yearning to make a larger contribution. Within several months the idea of doing the First Earth Run came back to David, and together we were ready to take it on.

For the next three years David and I had to use every empowerment tool we had ever learned or taught! My belief in myself was constantly stretched to the limits, as the magnitude of the vision often overwhelmed me. I just kept finding my next growing edge and working to affirm and visualize that I was capable enough to do this. The concept of trusting the universe jumped to a higher level of meaning for me during the Earth Run. I came to call this "radical trust." Radical trust meant that although I was putting my time, money, love, and personal reputation on the line, there was no guarantee that the event would work. All I had to sustain me was my trust.

Holding the First Earth Run fire, a participant in Lagos, Nigeria.

Ultimately, the First Earth Run was an opportunity to experience how much I had learned about personal growth and my ability to manifest. I used this knowledge in the most difficult and complex situations. I saw its power time and time again. Let me share with you some of my most precious experiences that made it all worth it:

In Burkina Faso, West Africa, one of the poorest countries on our planet, a crowd of 100,000 had come from hundreds of small villages to welcome the flame in the town of Bobo-Dioulasso. In an evening ceremony this enormous sea of African faces was illuminated by candles, which symbolized their hope for a peaceful world.

Gail and team members with Burkina Faso's president, Thomas Sankara.

David offering China's president, Li Xianan, the Torch of Peace in front of the Great Hall of People in Beijing.

In China, where the torch was welcomed by President Li Xianan, a million people gathered in Shanghai. We were welcomed into the Children's Palace by laughing children. We were enchanted. They led us into the outdoor courtyard where they taught us songs, dances, and games. I played patty-cake with a young Chinese girl who wore her hair in pigtails tied in enormous pink bows. In this moment I profoundly felt the precious joy of children and our responsibility to their future.

A Chinese torchbearer with the mayor of Beijing after many ascend to the top of the Great Wall of China to participate in the arrival of the Torch of Peace.

In Nicaragua, Ortega's child and the child of one of the Contra leaders walked together holding the torch while their fathers accompanied them. A cease-fire had been declared to allow for safe passage of the torch. What an unforgettable moment of hope!

President Corazon Aquino making an address to 600,000 Filipinos who have gathered to participate in the First Earth Run celebration in Manila.

In the Netherlands the torch journeyed to the Peace Palace at The Hague. The flame was accepted by World Court President Nagendra Singh and an eternal flame was lit by Prince Klaus. This ceremony was filled with an elegant dignity as we stood in a place consecrated to world peace, with people whose lives were dedicated to international justice and cooperation.

In the Soviet Union, where there was a strong message of support from Gorbachev, 100,000 people had gathered in Leningrad to welcome the flame. As we journeyed through the snowy streets hundreds of Soviets reached to grasp our hands and touch the torch in a powerful demonstration of friendship.

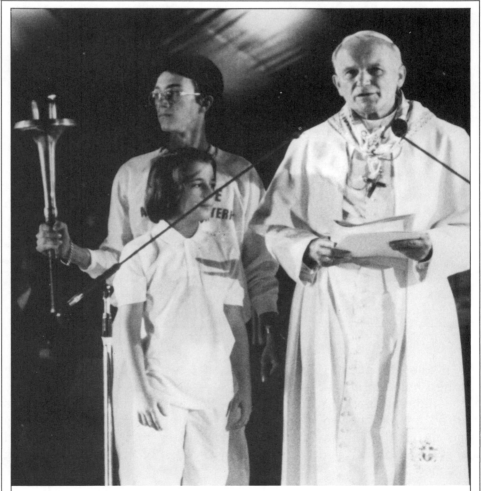

Pope John Paul II with the torch, speaking about peace and the world's youth at a large stadium gathering in Lyons, France.

In Indonesia, eight million people welcomed the torch during its five-day overland relay from Java to Bali. The flame, called the *Obor*, or friendship torch, was received with extraordinary joy and celebration as we witnessed the unforgettable music, dance, and spirit of the Indonesian people.

In India we were met by President Giani Zail Singh and were greeted with great enthusiasm in all cities to which we took the flame. In New Delhi we merged the flame of peace with Gandhi's eternal flame, placing a garland of marigolds on the sacred spot that honors him. In this poignant moment I completed the circle that had begun on that cold New Year's Day in 1983.

In Manama, the relaying of the torch by Ahmed Hamada, Bahrain's first gold medalist. Gail Straub is at his right.

On First Avenue in New York City, it began to snow as the torch returned home from its eighty-six-day odyssey. As we entered the lobby of the General Assembly Building, I was flooded with emotion as images from all around the world of hope, responsibility, joy, and possibility came racing through my consciousness. I knew that this journey had changed me forever, and I was awed by my love of this fragile, spinning ball called Earth.

What I learned from the Earth Run is that the challenges facing our world today are unsurpassed in complexity. I also know that we have tremendous untapped potential and creativity. I embrace this paradox, and I choose to act with hope as I wake each morning.

In closing we wish you much success in creating the life that you want. We also wish you much success in creating the kind of world you want to live in. Dream boldly—you have everything you need within you to fulfill your highest visions. We bid you farewell and blessings on your journey.

Further Support

Seminar Programs Available

Empowerment Workshop

Our personal growth training upon which this book was based. This three-and-a-half-day workshop is offered regularly throughout the United States and Europe. It provides you with an opportunity to take the work you have done in this book to the next level.

Art of Empowerment: A Professional Training in Facilitating Human Potential

Our professional development training program designed to assist professionals in becoming skillful in empowering others. It is appropriate for educators, organizational development trainers, health care professionals, managers, personal growth facilitators, therapists, group facilitators, and entrepreneurs.

Gaia Leadership: A Training for Transformational Change Agents

Our training program for those who recognize the essential interdependence between making ourselves more whole and making the world more whole—and are committed to both. This training program provides leadership and transformation skills within a global context for the individual called to action on behalf of planet Earth.

For a brochure or information on how to register for any of the above trainings, write:

Empowerment Training Programs
P.O. Box 417
West Hurley, New York 12491

Tapes and Books to Assist Your Personal Growth

Empowerment Audio Cassette Program—David Gershon and Gail Straub

An audio cassette program based on this book. It will elucidate the ideas of this book and give you an opportunity to be guided personally by us through the exercises and visualizations. Write to us at the above address for a brochure describing the program.

The Way of the Spiritual Warrior—David Gershon

An audio cassette on how to integrate a path of spirit with a path of action in the world. This live talk covers the qualities and training regimen of the spiritual warrior. The cost is $10 plus $1 for shipping and handling. You may order this tape directly by writing to the above address.

Soft Running: The Next Step—David Gershon

This book approaches the body in movement as an experience of play, dance, poetry, and consciousness expansion. It will assist you in taking the work you did in the body chapter to its next level. The cost is $10 plus $1 for shipping and handling. You may order this book directly by writing to the above address.

Bibliography of Some of Our Favorite Books

Metaphysics

Alexander, Thea. 2150 A.D. Warner Books.
Allen, James. As a Man Thinketh. Devorss & Co.
Bach, Richard. Illusions. Dell.
———. Jonathan Livingston Seagull. Dell.
———. The Bridge Across Forever. William Morrow & Co.
———. One. William Morrow & Co.
Dewey, Barbara. As You Believe. Bartholomew Books.
Gawain, Shakti. Creative Visualization. Whatever Publishing.
Hay, Louise. You Can Heal Your Life. Hay House.
Kueshana, Ekal. The Ultimate Frontier. Stelle Group.
Roberts, Jane. The Nature of Personal Reality: A Seth Book. Prentice-Hall.
———. The Individual and the Nature of Mass Events: A Seth Book. Prentice-Hall.
Spangler, David. The Laws of Manifestation. Findhorn.
Stack, Rick. Out of Body Adventures. Contemporary Books.

Relationships

Campbell, Susan. *The Couples Journey.* Impact Publications.
Lindthorst, Ann. *Marriage as a Spiritual Journey.* Paulist Press.
Mandel, Bob. *Open Heart Therapy.* Celestial Arts.
Ray, Sondra. *Loving Relationships.* Celestial Arts.
Satir, Virginia. *The New Peoplemaking.* Science and Behavior Books.
Ury, William, and Roger Fisher. *Getting to Yes.* Penguin.

Sexuality

Keen, Sam. *The Passionate Life: Stages of Loving.* Harper & Row.
Leonard, George. *The End of Sex: Erotic Love After the Sexual Revolution.* Tarcher.
Ross, William Ashoka. *Sex: There's More to It Than You've Been Told.* Playful Wisdom Press.
Weldwood, John. *Challenge of the Heart: Love, Sex, and Intimacy in Changing Times.* Shambhala.

The Body

Achterberg, Jeanne. *Imagery in Healing.* New Science Library.
Flugelman, Andrew. *The New Games Book.* Doubleday.
———. *More New Games.* Doubleday.
Gershon, David. *Soft Running: The Next Step.* Amity House.
Millman, Dan. *The Warrior Athlete: Body, Mind and Spirit.* Stillpoint.
Prudden, Susy. *Metafitness.* Hay House.
Ray, Sondra. *The Only Diet There Is.* Celestial Arts.
Sheehan, George. *How to Feel Great 24 Hours a Day.* Simon & Schuster.
Travis, John, and Regina Ryan. *Wellness Workbook: A Guide to Attaining High Level Wellness.* Ten Speed Press.

Money

Gilles, Jerry. *Moneylove.* Warner.
Phillips, Michael. *The Seven Laws of Money.* Random House.
Ponder, Catherine. *The Dynamic Laws of Prosperity.* Prentice-Hall.
Ross, Ruth. *Prospering Woman.* Whatever Publishing.

Work

Adams, John. *Transforming Work.* Miles River Press.
Bolles, Richard. *What Color Is Your Parachute?* Ten Speed Press.
Crystal, John. *Where Do I Go From Here With My Life?* Ten Speed Press.
Kamoroff, Bernard. *Small Time Operator.* Bell Springs Publishing.
Naisbitt, John, and Patricia Aburdene. *Re-inventing the Corporation.* Warner.
Phillips, Michael, and Salli Rasberry. *Honest Business.* Random House.
Ram, Dass, and Paul Gorman. *How Can I Help?* Alfred Knopf.
Sinetar, Marsha. *Do What You Love: The Money Will Follow.* Dell.

Spirituality

Castaneda, Carlos. *Tales of Power*. Simon & Schuster.

Emerson, Ralph Waldo. *Self-Reliance*. Peter Paul Press.

Faraday, Ann. *The Dream Game*. Perennial Library.

Fox, Matthew. *Original Blessing: A Primer in Creation Spirituality*. Bear & Co.

Jampolsky, Gerald. *Teach Only Love*. Bantam.

————. *Love Is Letting Go of Fear*. Bantam.

LaBerge, Stephen. *Lucid Dreaming*. Ballantine.

Levine, Stephen. *A Gradual Awakening*. Doubleday Anchor Press.

————. *Who Dies?* Doubleday Anchor Press.

————. *Healing into Life and Death*. Doubleday Anchor Press.

McLean, Dorothy. *To Hear the Angels Sing*. Lorian Press.

MacLaine, Shirley. *Dancing in the Light*. Bantam.

McLean, Dorothy. *To Hear the Angels Sing*. Lorian Press.

Nhat Hanh, Thich. *The Miracle of Mindfulness*. Beacon Press.

————. *Being Peace*. Parallax Press.

Pierrakos, Eva. *Guide Lectures for Self-Transformation*. Path Work Press.

Ram, Dass. *Journey of Awakening*. Bantam.

Rosanoff, Nancy. *Intuition Workout*. Aslan.

Swimme, Brian. *The Universe Is a Green Dragon*. Bear & Co.

Vaughan, Frances. *Awakening Intuition*. Doubleday Anchor.

Planet

Berry, Thomas. *The Dream of the Earth*. Sierra Club Books.

Carlson, Don, and Craig Comstock. *Citizen Summitry*. Tarcher.

————. *Securing Our Planet*. Tarcher.

Harmon, Willis. *Global Mind Change*. Knowledge Systems.

Henderson, Hazel. *Creating Alternative Futures*. Wideview/Perigree Books.

Hubbard, Barbara Marx. *The Evolutionary Journey*. Evolutionary Press.

Muller, Robert. *New Genesis: Shaping a Global Spirituality*. Doubleday.

Myers, Norman. *Gaia: An Atlas of Planet Management*. Doubleday Anchor.

Roszak, Theodore. *Person/Planet*. Doubleday Anchor Press.

Russell, Peter. *The Global Brain*. Tarcher.

Theobald, Robert. *The Rapids of Change*. Knowledge Systems.

Walsh, Roger. *Staying Alive: The Psychology of Human Survival*. New Science Library.

General Transformation

Campbell, Joseph. *The Power of Myth*. Doubleday.

Capra, Fritjof. *The Turning Point*. Bantam.

Elgin, Duane. *Voluntary Simplicity*. William Morrow.

Ferguson, Marilyn. *The Aquarian Conspiracy*. Tarcher.

Fields, Rick, and Peggy Taylor. *Chop Wood, Carry Water*. Tarcher.

Houston, Jean. *The Possible Human*. Tarcher.

Maslow, Abraham. *Towards a Psychology of Being*. Van Nostrand Reinhold.

About the Authors

David Gershon is leader and co-founder of the internationally acclaimed human potential training, the Empowerment Workshop, and offers management training and consulting to organizations throughout the world. He was director of the Olympic Torch Relay and conceived and was global organizer of the monumental world peace event, the First Earth Run, which had the participation of 25 million people and 45 heads of state in 62 countries. He is founder and president of the Gaia Leadership Project, an initiative to empower and align the leadership that is now being called to action on behalf of the planet.

Gail Straub is leader and co-founder of the Empowerment Workshop, an internationally recognized human potential training program, and has designed and led trainings for thousands of people worldwide. Gail was co-founder and international director of the First Earth Run, a major global initiative that took place in 1986 as part of the United Nations International Year of Peace. As a global citizen diplomat she has traveled and worked in over 50 countries, including two years in the Peace Corps in West Africa. She has designed citizen diplomacy projects between Chinese and American social innovators.